MATTHEW'S TRAVELS

10 YEARS OF TRIPS FOR 'THE TRAVEL SHOW'

Matthew Collins

Happy Travels Len best wishes, Matthew Collins

Published by:
MATC Publishing Ltd.
P.O. Box 11507
London
W14 9FX
United Kingdom

© Matthew Collins 1993, 1996, 1997, 1999

First Edition Published by MATC Publishing Ltd. 1993
Distributed by Ashford, Buchan & Enright

Reprinted 1994

Fourth Edition Published and Distributed by MATC Publishing Ltd. 1999

ISBN   0 9528553 1 3

Cartoons by Ted Spittles and David Fisher

Cover design theme, 'Holiday Snaps', by Publicity Project (Newbury) Ltd., Berkshire.

Cover Photographs

Front Cover	'Travelling Matthew' by Bryan Moody
	Minorca Beach supplied by World Pictures
Back Cover	Feature photographs by Matthew Collins
	'Khelga, Matthew and Charlie' by
	Bryan Moody

Printed and Bound by MPG Books, Bodmin, Cornwall.

To Anne, Pat, Jim, Pete and Dan.
And, of course, Khelga, Charlie and Nicolai.

CONTENTS

PART FOUR   A Few Favourite Countries and Memories

ACKNOWLEDGEMENTS

As usual, I am grateful to Richard Joseph for his publishing expertise and to Alison Howard for typesetting amendments.

This is the fourth edition of *Matthew's Travels* so I would like to thank all those people who bought the previous editions (and thank you for buying this one).

Just in case you haven't heard about it, may I tell you about my other book *Across America with the boys*. It's the story of my biggest ever travel challenge – an eleven week trip across the States in a motorhome made with my two small children *while my wife stayed behind to start a new career*. I promise it's an entertaining (and informative) read.

I do hope you enjoy this book. If you have any comments, suggestions (or work offers) at all, please don't hesitate to get in touch – at the MATC Publishing e-mail (matcltd@aol.com) or postal address (on title page).

Happy travels. Best wishes.

Matthew Collins

London 1999

PART ONE

The Most Challenging Challenges

A PERMANENT VACATION

'So what's it like being on permanent vacation? And getting paid at the same time?'

I was in Alaska, in Beluga, a small settlement 65 miles north of Anchorage. The man asking the question was Dennis Torrey, known by locals as the Wild Man. I was about to fire his .44 Magnum.

'Well, my trips aren't exactly all holidays,' I said. It was a question I had been asked a thousand times. 'Each week on the programme they give me a travel challenge. This Alaska trip was a challenge but it was easy. Some of them have proved rather difficult.'

Bham! The bullet hit the oil barrel and split it in two. 'Neat shot Matt. Not bad for your first time with a Magnum. So tell me about some of these travel challenges. . .'

*   *   *

CHAPTER ONE

A Week Alone in a French Nudist Camp

'Now this week, Matthew,' said Paul Heiney, then 'The Travel Show's' main presenter, 'you're off to France, – to the breezy Atlantic west coast. I hope it's not too breezy because you're going to be staying... IN A NUDIST CAMP. You won't need to pack. But don't forget the suncream. Good luck. Come back and tell us all about the experience next week.'

Numb with shock I flew to Bordeaux, picked up a hire car and began my drive west to the nudist camp.

After an hour I came to a forest and soon began to see small *'Centre Naturiste'* signs on arrows. I followed them, driving deeper through pine trees. I came to a security gate, the first of three, which I passed through feeling nervous and excited.

By the time I'd reached the third gate I was quivering like an adolescent schoolboy. I showed all my tickets and looked out for my first real, live nudists. Suddenly it started to rain.

'Damn,' I thought, 'They'll all be running back to put their clothes on.'

But little did I know that when naturists have come on holiday to be naked they're never put off by a shower. So the first nudists I saw were a Swedish family wearing hooded waterproofs – except from the waist down they had nothing on at all. And the second group I saw were half a dozen Germans, quite starkers but holding umbrellas – although some of them had shoes on too.

I took a deep gulp. The nudism was for real. And I was going to have to join in.

I picked up the key and went to my chalet. A list of regulations accompanied the leaflets I'd collected. My eyes immediately fixed on rule one: 'Nudity is obligatory at all times.'

I dumped my small case, went on to my terrace and waved to my nude German neighbours. I was still wearing my shorts.

Time for a swim. I went to the pool. The changing room came as a shock – it was mixed (and used mainly for taking off shoes). I slid off my shorts, dived into the water and, despite my British modesty, came to the conclusion that a swim in the nude really was more pleasurable than with trunks. But I wasn't completely liberated yet. So once out of the pool my shorts went on quickly again.

Next stop was the 'Centre Commercial.' This had a bank, where nudists were cashing their travellers' cheques; a restaurant and café, where nudists were eating and drinking; and a supermarket, where nudists were shopping.

I popped in to buy some provisions. A 75-year-old lady rushed up to me. She was a disconcerting sight. She was naked of course. I felt awkward standing in front of her.

'It's Matthew, isn't it? Is this where they've sent you this week? Well, good for them. How are you enjoying it? You've got to get those shorts off you know... well maybe not here as it does get a bit cold when you go past the freezers. But if you want to be accepted you can't have your clothes on. How long are you staying for anyway?'

She called over her husband – he must have been 80. He was wearing only plimsolls and a cap. 'Hey Arthur. You recognise this young chap don't you? It's Matthew from the telly. They've sent him to be a naturist this week.'

'Oh yes... Hello Matthew. Pleased to meet you.' And he held out his hand for me to shake.

Arthur and Marjorie then introduced me to two younger, 60ish-year-old friends of theirs, Tom and Hilary. They were also naked and were buying some salami at the deli. To my astonishment Tom had a false leg.

When we'd all finished shopping we went to the café for a drink.

'Well I've been a naturist since before the war,' said Arthur. 'The thing about naturism is that it equalises everything. You may think that's funny. But in this place we've got managing directors and shop-floor workers and nobody can tell the difference between them. They take off their status when they take off their clothes and leave their self-consciousness behind.'

'And the other thing, Matthew,' said Hilary, 'is that nudity actually de-sexualises the body. You take a woman in a skimpily cut bikini — well she's far more provocative than a nudist. It's only because of the way we're brought up that we associate nudity with sex. In native tribes they don't have that problem. And nor do you here after a while — there's a limit to how long you can go on associating nudity with sex.'

'And what's more,' said Tom, 'bodies become less important. That may surprise you. But nobody pays attention to them here. My artificial leg gets far more attention at home in the pub than it does here when I walk round unclothed.'

After my introduction to nudist philosophy I rushed off to my room to phone some friends. 'It's weird,' I told my girl-friend Amanda. 'It's full of nutters. And it's worse being here on my own. Why don't you come down for the weekend? Or take a week off work? I'll pay for your ticket. You'll have great food and wine. And we don't even have to spend much time here.'

She said that unfortunately she was busy.

I phoned up some other friends and asked them to come but they said they couldn't make it either. Then I tried a friend in Paris — she was busy too — and remembered that I knew a girl near Nantes. 'It's a great place,' I said. 'Everyone's friendly and the beach is just wonderful.' But she said she couldn't come down either.

When I went for my next walk I met yet another English couple.

'I'm Michael and this is my wife Deborah and these are our children Benjamin and Flora.'

They were both in their late thirties and had been coming to the same camp for years.

'So you haven't taken the plunge yet,' said Deborah, pointing to my shorts.

'No, not yet,' I admitted. 'But I did have a swim in the pool.'

'And didn't you feel better for it?' said Michael. 'I don't know how men swim in trunks.'

They were very friendly and could see that I was nervous so they invited me to dinner at their caravan.

When I arrived, a couple of hours later, Deborah was outside, stirring some soup. It was in a pot, on a burner, on a small camping table and there were food stains all over her breasts.

Michael, who was also naked, was seeing to the wine for the meal. The bottle was nestled in his plump, hairy legs. Plop! The cork came out. He grinned happily. He held up his goblet and slurped. 'Red all right, Matthew?' He winked in approval. He looked like a naughty Greek satyr.

'What do you do for a living, Mike?' I asked.

'Oh, I'm a bank manager,' he replied.

'And what about you, Deborah?'

'I'm a history teacher in a boys' school.'

By now her breasts were covered in still more soup.

The kids who'd been sitting on a blanket were ordered by Mike to lay the table. 'They're off to a disco later on,' he said, 'So they won't be hanging round here long.'

'Was the disco a... um... naked disco?' I asked.

'Well, not necessarily,' said Mike, 'Clothes optional really. I mean they'll dress up if it gets a bit chilly. Basically you can do what you want.'

'So do you think I could stay without ever taking all my clothes off?'

'Possibly,' he said. 'But don't forget – the whole point of coming here is to be naked. And if people start noticing that you never are, they might get a little suspicious. Especially,' he added with caution, 'as you're a man on your own. I don't know how they arranged that. Because usually single men are banned here. For obvious reasons of course.'

'Of course,' I said.

After the soup the main course was chicken. Mike carved. It looked slightly dangerous.

'Voilà,' he said. 'Poulet rôti à l'Anglaise.'

We talked about a lot of things during the meal – cricket, Ian Botham, the price of the pound. Everything was normal – except that I was the only one wearing clothes.

The children went off to their disco.

Later I learnt that none of their 'textile' friends knew Mike and Deborah were nudists. 'Textiles' are what naturists call non-nudists: people who wear clothes – or rather people who like to wear

clothes on holiday. Mike said it was too risky to tell any 'textiles' in case the bank ever found out.

For them both, going away meant relaxing completely and the best way to do that was to spend their time naked. Nudity gave them complete freedom — from not having to worry about what to wear, to enjoying all the elements — sun, wind and rain — over every single inch of their bodies.

He was also pleased that the kids were growing up without any hang-ups about nudity. 'The only problem is in P.E. when they go back to school. They have to be careful in the showers — if the other kids see they've got an all-over sun-tan they could twig their family were naturists.'

At the end of the evening I thanked Mike and Deborah and made my way back to my chalet.

'And get those shorts off,' Deborah called. 'You'll feel much more normal here. And then you can start to enjoy it.'

The following morning I met two more neighbours — German girls who both looked the same. They can't have been more than 16.

'We're twins. I'm Ingrid.'

'And my name is Silke.'

'My name is Matthew,' I said.

The girls were very pretty. It was almost as much as I could do to say hello before I felt I had to go back inside. But suddenly I had an idea.

One of my 'Travel Show' problems was that I was always alone with a video or camera and had to ask people I met on my trips to take different pictures of me. At times this was extremely difficult and I'd known that this camp would be a problem.

The idea of approaching strange naked people and asking them to take NUDE shots of me was almost too embarrassing to imagine. And when I saw signs saying 'Photography Forbidden' I thought it would be practically impossible.

But these two young German girls seemed the solution. I told them I worked for BBC television and was doing a report for a holiday programme. They looked pretty sceptical but I carried on talking.

'You see, I always travel alone. I'm a reporter but I don't have a photographer and I need to have pictures of myself. I was just wondering if you wouldn't mind taking a few pictures of me – just to prove I was here.'

They looked at each other and seemed to say 'why not?'

'Okay,' said Ingrid, 'Where would you like us to take them?'

Five minutes later we were all on a quiet patch of beach. Silke and Ingrid each had a camera and I was in the sea, naked as the day I was born.

With my hands carefully placed I turned to the girls and smiled a silly grin for the cameras. 'Take loads of pictures. Don't worry about film. I've got loads more of that in my bag.' And as Ingrid and Silke tried out new angles, I tried out lots of different poses.

I ran through the sea, I dived in the surf, I grinned, I looked serious and I even turned round to show my bottom. (I thought rear shots might be more broadcastable – we were, after all, on before 9 p.m.) 'Did you get that one Silke? That was quite funny.' Soon the girls were getting more ambitious.

Silke started zooming in on some shots and coming very close for the others. Ingrid ran around and just kept her finger on the shutter button.

Suddenly there was a loud Germanic shout

'Vot are you doing?' It was the father of Silke and Ingrid.

I explained to him I worked for the BBC, that I was doing a report on the naturist centre and that I needed some shots of myself here.

He then asked what I thought a pretty stupid question: 'So — where is your identity please?'

'Well I don't have it at the moment I'm afraid. I don't actually have any clothes on.'

He summoned the girls and told me that I had 'von hell of a lot of explaining to do'.

Back in my chalet the phone rang. It was the manager of the camp. 'Monsieur Collins — I'm afraid we've had a complaint. A guest says you've been corrupting his daughters. Something about pictures in the sea. Would you come over to my office *s'il vous plaît.*'

I couldn't believe it. I'd always known that this assignment would be difficult.

The girls' father had accused me of being a menace and had demanded that I be thrown off the camp. I explained why I'd been taking the pictures and asked the manager if he could explain this to the German man.

The manager said that naturist centres always had to be careful about photography. I told him that the photos of me were a necessary part of my report. He said okay but asked me to be discreet and suggested I find older guests to take them. Then I explained that photos of me weren't the only problem — I also needed shots of other people. He frowned, took a deep breath and thought for a while, then proposed a public announcement. 'Maybe we could ask for volunteers. Tell people you need to take pictures and that, if they agree to pose, they might be on TV in Britain.'

That sounded good. It would certainly give me more credibility. I agreed immediately and he made the announcement over the naturist centre's PA. The result was fantastic. Only minutes later two volunteers were knocking at my chalet door.

'*Bonjour,*' said one of the French girls, 'We heard you were looking for models. You want us to pose for your programme?'

'Well that might be a good idea... I suppose so — yes please.'

'You want us both naked?'

'Well definitely... I'll just get my cameras. Wait a second. Don't go away.'

In a flash I was back on the beach. This was the kind of job I'd always wanted. 'Okay Chantal, just run towards me again... Now Hélène, let's do a few more on the bicycle.'

By the end of the week I'd used 15 films and had over 500 shots in the bag. I'd never had such fun in my life. This nudist camp was my best assignment yet I thought.

Apart from the announcement, things really improved from the moment I finally dropped my shorts. Suddenly I was a member of the great big friendly naturist family. I made friends everywhere and the camaraderie really was overwhelming.

A few people resented my presence but I never took unwanted photos. Most people were only too happy to be photographed without any clothes on – doing their *danse libre* in the fields (naked breathing exercises with mime – very popular with the older German ladies); going for a jog round the camp (the men wore swimming trunks – the women just a bra); playing with bows and arrows in the woods (the men looked like x-rated Robin Hoods); making clay pots in the craft shop (nudists sat at little potters' wheels); or just going round the camp on bicycles.

Although most of the guests were German (followed closely by the Swedes then the French) I kept bumping into English people (no Irish, Welsh or Scots though – nudity is obviously not for Celts). The friendliness seemed to prove that nudity really did perform a social function in breaking down people's reserve. But I did find it quite disconcerting when people came up to me and said: 'It's Matthew from the television, isn't it? Yes, I thought I recognised you,' and I was standing there starkers. Which part of me had they recognised? I soon felt self-conscious again.

I can't say I'll ever become a proper nudist – somehow it just didn't feel natural and despite the friendly attitudes I found myself wanting more privacy. I haven't been on a naturist holiday since but did greatly appreciate some aspects of life at the camp.

It wasn't long before I'd acquired the very pleasant naturist habit of waking up in the morning and getting up without getting dressed. No worries about clean socks or underpants or what clothes I'd wear each day. I'd just get up, jump on my bicycle (which had a little towel wrapped round the saddle for extra comfort) and cycle off in the nude to the camp-site *boulangerie* to buy my tasty, fresh, French *baguette*.

I'd have breakfast on my terrace (the crumbs were sometimes a little irritating), pedal off to the beach and swim for an hour, before going off to meet some of my many new-found nudist friends.

There were loads of them and as well as having plenty of models at my disposal – young and old, male and female, all nationalities (but not the bank manager and his wife) – I found a wonderful photographer to take all the pictures of me. Marie-Françoise was a sociology student from Biarritz and had written a thesis on 'The Social Potential of Integrated Naturism in France'. She lent me a copy – it was absolute nonsense – but the pictures she took were always perfectly focused and exposed.

As I said, I had over 500 shots by the end of the week, but when I got back to Manchester my excitement was tempered – they couldn't use most of those I'd taken. 'Just a bit well... you know...' said the producer. 'Nine o'clock watershed and all that...'

I thought they were all extremely harmless but they carefully selected a few of the more obviously innocent ones – couples in the restaurants, nudists pushing supermarket trolleys, and used some of those of me taken by the two German girls.

Naturally I gave the nudist camp a balanced report – I was very fair and didn't mock it – and as a result of explaining the nudist philosophy I endeared myself to naturists in Britain. They all thought they had a friend on TV sympathetic to the naturist cause

That wasn't quite the case but nevertheless, following the programme, I was bombarded with invitations and literature – 'You are cordially invited to a naturist barbeque in Bristol'. 'Come to a naturist disco in Leicester'. I also received magazines and guides.

For years afterwards I continued to receive naturist bumf and every summer a gentleman called Phil Vallack sent me his *Free Sun* publications.

Phil is a very endearing, retired art teacher and his *Free Sun* publications are guides to the nudist beaches in Europe. He used to research, write, design and lay them out himself in his house garage in Hastings. He's stopped producing them now but I've got a stack on my shelves and one day one really came in handy (I'll explain more in a later chapter).

The naturist magazines are funny things. I'm not talking about products like *Health and Efficiency* but about Naturist Clubs' own publications. Some of them have the strangest small ads. I was reading one the other day. It went: 'Bill and Tina are now happy to offer their solar-heated Milton Keynes home up for naturist bed and breakfast for businessmen. £20 a night. Contact Box XX.' So if ever you're doing business in Milton Keynes and are looking for a naturist B and B I'll dig up the box number for you.

But there's another, more embarrassing follow-up to this story.

A few days after my nudist camp report I was on the London Underground travelling on a Central Line train. It was eight-thirty, on a miserable Monday morning and I was going from Ealing Broadway to Bank. The carriage was stuffed with people and, as usual on a rush-hour tube, the atmosphere was profoundly depressing.

No one was talking and everyone was minding their own business. Those lucky enough to have a seat were hiding their faces behind papers. The rest of the passengers were trying to stand up, hanging on to springy handles like baboons. Everyone looked vacant and detached.

At each stop further east the train got more full. At Holborn a group of tourists and office workers came aboard, at St Paul's a couple of smart businessmen. Finally, when the carriage was about to burst, a traditional city gent got on. He was pin-striped, bowler-hatted, carrying a brolly and must have been an old-school stockbroker.

Just before Bank we got stuck in a tunnel. The engine went dead. There was silence. The minutes passed by, the train didn't move and the tension became more and more unbearable. Suddenly the stockbroker smiled and winked at me. I looked away, not to show interest. But a voice crisply shattered the silence: 'I must say,' he said. 'I think you've got a very lovely bottom!'

'Thank you,' I said. Presumably he'd seen 'The Travel Show' that week.

CHAPTER TWO

The Leg-in-Plaster Trip Down to Spain.

The following summer the producer of 'The Travel Show' threw me another real wobbler. By now I had tackled all kinds of trips but nothing could have ever prepared me for such an extraordinary challenge.

'Now, Matthew, this week's assignment... Unfortunately some people have accidents just before they go away on holiday...'

I started to panic.

'What happens if you break your leg for example? Can you still travel? Can you still have a good time?..'

My face looked puzzled and vexed...

'Matthew... please meet Sister Birch...'

Before I had time to protest Sister Birch pushed me on to a stretcher, her colleague Pam ripped off my trousers and both of the nurses went to work putting plaster on my perfectly healthy right leg.

'Yes, Matthew I'm afraid you're going away with a pretend broken femur this week. Your right leg's going to be plastered – from your toes to your thigh – and then you're going on a journey. Keep putting on the plaster of Paris nurse. We'll come back to you later in the programme.'

Half an hour later I was still lying on the stretcher. My right leg was totally encased, and Paul Heiney was giving me my tickets.

'Now, Matthew, you're going down to Spain. We want you to see with firsthand experience what travelling facilities for the disabled are like. And just to make it interesting we want you to travel overland. From Manchester you'll be taking the coach to London, and from London the train to Dover. At Dover we want you to catch the hovercraft to Boulogne and then you take the train down to Paris. At Paris you change stations – you'll have to cross the city – and then you take the train down to Spain. Finally at Blanes you take a bus and travel into Lloret de Mar. You're booked into a hotel and you'll have 48 hours to soak up the sun before you catch your flight back to Gatwick. Good luck, take it easy and tell us all about it next week...'

As the credits rolled an instant cripple hobbled out of Studio B.

That night the programme put me up in the Midland, one of Manchester's smartest hotels. 'We thought you deserved a bit of comfort,' said the producer. (Before then I'd always stayed with friends.) I had dinner with some of 'The Travel Show' team and then went up to bed.

Unfortunately after all the excitement I'd drunk a whole bottle of wine. My room was on the first floor but instead of taking the lift I decided I'd try out the stairs.

For the first few steps I did really well – putting my good leg on each new step then lifting my plastered one round. But suddenly I lost my balance. The weight of the plaster pulled me down and I crashed to the bottom in a heap.

Luckily I hadn't been high up. People in the lobby all turned and stared. A porter rushed over to help. I was more embarrassed than bruised, but my plaster cast had cracked at the knee.

'Oh wonderful,' I thought, as I bent it. 'Things will be easier now.' And after saying goodnight again I got in the lift and went up to bed feeling great.

I didn't expect an alarm call next morning. It was the programme producer.

'I hear you've broken your cast.'

'Not much,' I said, 'just a little crack. It hardly makes any difference.'

'Get down to the Infirmary immediately. You'll have to have a new one put on. Your coach leaves at 10.30 so you've got enough time. And I want you to come up to my office so I can check the plaster's okay. I don't want you cheating. See you in an hour. I'll ring up the hospital now.'

So with hardly any time to have breakfast, I rushed out to get a new cast. Sister Birch's colleague, Pam, was there. And to make sure the same thing didn't happen again she put on an extra thick layer.

My trip down to Spain got off to a very easy start.

On the coach to London I met a 70-year-old lady called Alice who let me put my leg on her lap. (She had the honour of signing my cast first.)

At Victoria I had a pleasant surprise – a courier with a wheelchair was there to meet me and he took me to the train station shuttle. 'Oh yes, this is normal service,' he said. 'Trouble is lots of old dears take advantage of it. They find out about wheelchairs and have one arranged every trip even though they're not really disabled. We get to recognise the faces.'

At Dover I was met by another smiling courier and on the hovercraft given two seats. And at Boulogne where I was helped to disembark first, there was yet another wheelchair waiting.

All sympathy ended in Paris at the Gare du Nord. There was no courier and no wheelchair. It was 10 p.m., pouring with rain and there were no departures for Spain until the morning.

Luckily I'd made a friend on the train from Boulogne. Ross was 18 and travelling in Europe for the first time. He was on his way to Greece, but as he was staying in Paris for the night we decided to find a hotel together.

The Gare du Nord is near Pigalle, the red-light district of Paris. We traipsed past the peep-shows getting soaked by the rain as we tried to find a cheap room. By the time we'd found one (on the fifth floor) my plaster was sodden and my naked toes, which peeked from the end, felt like they were going to rot.

Fortunately for me, Ross turned out to be a highly organised young chap. Even though he was going to Greece he'd packed a hairdrier in his rucksack. He ripped off the British plug, stuffed the bare wires into a socket and gave my plastered leg a quick blow-dry. Ross turned out to be so well organised he also had a thick plastic sack ('I thought it might be useful in an emergency'). So before going for something to eat he covered up my leg and fastened it with four elastic bands – he even supplied those as well.

We'd just left our room when a young girl jumped out in front of us. 'Are you American? Are you English? Can I come and speak with you? These men here are driving me crazy. They won't stop knocking on my door. They're all convinced I'm a prostitute.' She tagged along with us to a restaurant.

Helena, who was from Sweden, was Inter-railing on her own and regretting it. She was a nurse from Gothenburg and after the meal she insisted on massaging my foot. 'But they are mad to do this to you. What do you mean it's not broken? You could get terrible gangrene.' She made me promise I would go straight to a hospital the moment my foot turned blue.

Although I got the sympathy, Ross got the girl. Helena took a shine to his youthful Scottish innocence and that night they decided to travel down to Italy together. (Two weeks later I received a card from Ross in Rome saying he'd never made it to Greece.)

The next day we all had breakfast and as the happy couple boarded their train I limped off to see Paris. I headed for Beaubourg and walked around but it wasn't much fun hobbling through Paris alone. Taxis refused me and the only concession was on the Metro where I could sit on seats reserved for the handicapped.

I sat down for a coffee at the trendiest café in Paris, Café Costes on the Rue de Rivoli. A waiter tripped over my cast. He snarled while the other customers smirked.

At the Gare Austerlitz later that afternoon the SNCF lady promised me a wheelchair for Spain.

But 12 hours later after a night in a sweaty couchette the wheelchair didn't materialise. I struggled down the platform with my luggage. I had two more trains, then a bus.

Thanks to a language problem, some nuns on the first train thought I was a professional 'futbolista'. They took it in turns to sign my cast and announced it to the rest of the passengers. One boy asked if I knew Gary Linekar and another said he'd seen Tottenham Hotspur play.

I arrived in Lloret at midday and checked into the hotel. My room was on the eighth floor, so I asked for another one, but they said, unconcerned, that they were full. I went to find a quick spot of lunch.

In a small local tapas bar I had *gambas al ajillo* (prawns in garlic), *ensalada Rusa* (Russian salad) and *huevos y gambas en la plancha con patatas* (fried eggs and prawns with potatoes).

Half an hour later I was back in my room when suddenly I felt a slight twinge. The prawns had sent my bowels into overdrive.

Diarrhoea is bad enough at the best of times but with your leg in a rigid plaster cast things become even more difficult. For the next three hours I panic-crashed my way through my bedroom as I limped from the bathroom to the bed.

Finally the calm came and I fell into a merciful sleep.

A few hours later I was woken by a voice screaming through the thin plaster wall.

'MORE...! Oh yes, Jimmy! Please Jimmy baby don't stop!'

She banged on the wall as Jim carried on. Her screams became louder. Jim started grunting. The bed squeaked, the floor shook... and I had a big twinge again.

When I'd finished in the bathroom, I banged on the wall. They didn't seem to hear so I put in my ear plugs. Finally I got back out of bed and gave the wall a kick with my cast.

Jim got the message and I fell asleep but at 5 o'clock that morning I was woken again. This time the noise was from a group of Geordie lads who, on their way home from the bars, had decided to serenade some girls in another room near to mine.

A chorus of Newcastle accents chimed out in the warm Spanish dawn: 'Get your bumps out, get your bumps out, get your buuu... mmmmmppppps... ow-ow-ow... out. Get your bumps out, get your bumps out, get your bumps ow-ow-ow out...'

'Come on Tricia, show us your tits!' shrieked one of the lads more directly. The rest of the group howled. There was laughter and cheering and wolf-whistles filled the air.

I now knew why the producer had booked me into this particular

23

hotel. He had just wanted to add to my challenge. I later learnt that this was an infamous hotel and had a reputation for mayhem and loudness.

When I went down to breakfast I felt unrefreshed, delicate and bleary-eyed. An old lady pushed across me as I limped to the queue for my cornflakes. 'What happened to you then, darling? Fall off your balcony did you?' She went off with a plateful of scrambled eggs and bacon muttering about booze and the sun.

By the time I reached the swimming pool all the sun-beds had been taken. I spread my towel out on a small piece of terrace and lay down with my crutches to sunbathe. I was beautifully relaxed when a small boy suddenly started to talk to me.

'Excuse me,' he said. 'Are you Matthew Collins?'

'Yes I am,' I replied.

Suddenly the whole family appeared. 'I knew it was him,' said the mother. 'Michael, ask him for his autograph. Quick Edward, go and get the camera.'

Edward waddled off to the family's little corner and returned with the Kodak Instamatic.

'You don't mind, do you,' said the mother squeezing herself onto my towel. 'Come on then, Michael, get next to Matthew. And you too Mum. Now, Edward, you can take the picture.'

Edward obliged and just as the shutter went off, the mother picked up one of my crutches and put her big arm round my neck. 'Oh thanks a million Matthew. Can I have another autograph for my sister? She'll never believe that we've met you. We saw you get your plaster on Thursday. Did you have a good journey? How do you like the hotel?'

I told her it was absolutely marvellous.

When I went to go back to my room the lift was out of order. 'Excuse me,' I said to the receptionist. 'When's the lift going to be mended? My room's on the eighth floor. How am I going to reach it with this?'

She looked over the counter at my leg. 'I'm very sorry. We can't get a repairman until tomorrow. I'm afraid you'll have to walk.'

With my towel, my crutches and a bottle of Ambre Solaire, I began the ascent to my room. By the sixth floor I was completely out of breath. Suddenly a stampede nearly knocked me over. Three burly figures racing down the stairs careered past me, knocking down a crutch.

They were the Newcastle boys who'd been singing outside.

'Oh my God!' said the biggest one, coming back to pick up the crutch. 'You're that bloke on the telly. The one they send off everywhere. Martin, Michael... whasyername? Oy, Kevin, Richard come back here.' He called to his mates and they both returned to have a good look.

Despite their offensive singing they turned out to be good guys. They carried my crutches up to my room, offered me help getting down to dinner and even hung around two days later when I boarded a coach to connect with the plane home from Reus Airport.

I spent the remaining time trying to relax as best I could. But time dragged — sunbathing was a challenge, discos were difficult and there wasn't much else to do in Lloret.

Finally I was on my way home and looking forward to getting my plaster off. The return journey turned out to be much easier than the outward one. I got on the plane and once we were airborne the pilot radioed Gatwick and told them he had an invalid on board.

I couldn't have asked for a better reception than the one I got at Gatwick. An American-style motorised golf buggy rushed me to the front of the passport queue. I was whizzed through immigration, my suitcase was collected, then the driver whisked me through customs.

All special treatment ended at the Gatwick Airport taxi rank when a cabbie told me a ride back to Walthamstow would not cost less than £50.

I told him I only had £20. 'Well, you better get the train mate,' he said. I hobbled off to the Gatwick Express, took the tube at Victoria, had a night at home in London and then went up to Manchester on the train to do the programme next day.

In those days it was live and went out at 8.30 p.m. The producer wanted me to do it with my leg still encased in its cast, so my freedom had to wait still longer.

'How much will you give me to let you have it off?' said Paul Heiney live on air when I'd finished my report.

'I'm going to have it off the moment I get out of here,' I replied. And as the credits rolled, I limped out of the studio, jumped in a taxi and raced off to Manchester Infirmary.

At nine fifty-five Sister Pam cut off my cast. I got off the bed, tried to stand up but collapsed like a newly born foal. My leg would no longer support me. It had withered in just a few days.

CHAPTER THREE

The Cruellest Trip

After travelling South through Europe with my right leg in a plaster cast when it was not even broken, I thought I had been the fall guy for ALL the producer's evil ideas, but only a couple of weeks later he had another really cruel one up his sleeves.

'For this week's assignment Matthew, you're going to be taking a coach. We want you to see what LONG-DISTANCE coach trips are like... so you're going to be travelling down to Athens...

'It takes 70 hours to get there so you should arrive late Monday morning. Two hours later, on Monday afternoon, you'll be on your way home... but I'm afraid this will also be by coach.

'You'll have six days and six nights of travelling altogether, so don't forget to take things to read. Come back next week and tell us about the joys and some of the perils of spending a week on a coach...'

That really was the worst assignment I ever had.

To make things even more worrying I soon discovered I was travelling with a company called 'Miracle Bus'.

The coach was departing from Camden, although when I arrived at the little backstreet it had all the atmosphere of a Greek dockyard just before the departure of a liner. Families were shouting, lovers were crying, old men embraced and shook hands. Finally the engine was started and we steamed on to the A2 for Dover.

It was hard to spot any obvious tourists on board. There were two Australians and a couple of English boys. But the rest were Greeks or Cypriots returning home from London for the summer. For the first hour of our journey I couldn't stop thinking, 'Why don't they just take a flight?'.

The reason, for most, I discovered, was that the coach let them take much more luggage. Whereas on an aeroplane most people check in one suitcase, some people here were checking in five or six bags. One woman even seemed to have dozens – I later learnt that she had sold her house in London and was going home to Greece to retire. There were other advantages as well – itineraries were more flexible, they could spend more time on holiday (the usual limit on a charter flight was just a few weeks) and some, of course, were terrified of flying.

We cruised through Kent but already it felt more like Greece. There were Greek songs on the stereo, Greek films on the video, and most of the conversation around me was in Greek. I was sitting next to George Bratsioti, a Paddington-based student who'd made the journey several times before. George had come well-prepared with three five-litre bottles of mineral water (and a cooler), dozens of cheese and ham sandwiches and 20 cassettes for his Walkman.

But other passengers were also well-equipped. One old hand – a Liverpudlian lady, married to a Greek, travelling with four small children – had spent £25 in Kwik Save on provisions. 'What did you buy?' I asked her.

'Oh, the usual,' she said. 'Crisps, Coke, water, bread, and half a dozen cans of Irish stew.' Did she have a stove? 'Don't need one. By the time we get to Munich the cans are all so hot that when you open them the stew is almost boiling.'

We reached Munich the following day. The stew was indeed almost boiling. So were the passengers. The pace of the trip was relentless. There were no loos on board and our only opportunities for relief came every three hours when one of the two Greek drivers pulled into a service station and shouted 'Okay – 10 minutes toilet.' The other one then shouted 'Hurry up please!' as stragglers made it back to the bus.

Before the trip I'd heard all kinds of horror stories about coach trips to Athens involving *ouzo*-swilling drivers careering along unmade Yugoslavian roads at 100 m.p.h. But our men were reassuringly sensible. They stuck to the speed limits and their only drink was coffee. The one slightly worrying thing was that they usually relaxed in the luggage compartment of the coach – they had a camp-bed down there (I suppose it was the only place they could lie flat) so every six hours they'd swop over driving and crawl in with the cases for a sleep.

By day three we were in what was then Yugoslavia. The quality of the roads and service stations was poor. It was hot and clammy and no one on board had had a proper wash. The Liverpudlian lady with the Irish stew was still serving portions to her kids and I was regretting that I hadn't stocked up as well. The choice of the food in the service stations was awful — endless very stale and crusty pastries. I couldn't work out any of the currency and I already had a pocket of useless small change from the stops in Germany and Austria.

The trip through Yugoslavia seemed interminable and I was unable to sleep. For the first 24 hours of the journey I'd had an inflatable neck pillow (marvellous for coach journeys — I highly recommend them) but unfortunately this had burst in Austria. I tried to wedge a T-shirt between the window and my head but this didn't stop it vibrating.

At least George Bratsioti turned out to be a nice chap. He gave me the odd sandwich and told me all about his family in Athens and his Swedish girl-friend in London. Then he invited me to stay with them in Naxos (he refused to believe I had only two hours in Athens before taking another coach home). As well as his sandwiches, he shared his Walkman. We both stuffed an ear-piece in one ear and tried to doze off to Phil Collins. Luckily Phil did the trick and successfully lulled me to sleep. But suddenly I was woken by shouting. There was loud clapping, cheering and excitement. It was four in the morning, we'd crossed the Greek border and were in Thessaloniki.

We stopped at a roadside taverna and everyone trooped out to celebrate. Even the lady with the Irish stew splashed out on a slap-up family meal — *souvlaki* and *ouzo* for herself, Cokes and *baklava* for the kids.

The last stop was at eight, but few passengers were interested in breakfast. Most were more concerned with sprucing themselves up for the benefit of people meeting them in Athens. There were queues by the luggage hold as clean outfits were pulled out of cases, and passengers went off with plastic water bottles to attempt a crude wash or a shave.

We arrived in Athens at 11 o'clock, only half an hour late and pretty good considering we'd been on the road for three days. But the slight delay had a magnified importance for me — it meant I only had a 90-minute break instead of a two-hour rest in Athens. But when I got off the coach I was almost glad to be leaving straight away.

Athens was suffering one of its worst heat waves for decades — the temperature was 45°C and rising. People were dying on the streets and one of the other bus stations had been turned into a mortuary because all the proper ones were full.

I was determined however that I'd still see the Parthenon and that I'd have a quick stuffed pepper in a restaurant. But then I couldn't get a taxi — they were all on strike — so I settled for a take-away near the bus garage. I'd hardly finished when it was time to board the coach home.

It was a different bus company, and this time, instead of Greeks, the passengers were young northern Europeans. I sat at the back in the middle (where there was more leg room) between two English students who'd spent six months in Egypt, a German girl who'd left her Greek boy-friend in Mykonos, and two other German girls who were taking theirs home to meet mother.

We shared cans of tuna fish through Yugoslavia and then changed coaches in Munich. As we went further north the bus made more regular stops. The young travellers got off and cleaner, fresher passengers got on.

By the time we reached Brussels the English students and I were the only originals on board. We arrived at Victoria on Thursday. I was exhausted. I took the train to Manchester, did the programme that night, and was in Sicily for 'The Travel Show' next day. I did NOT travel to Palermo by coach.

PART TWO

How The Travel Bug Bit

CHAPTER FOUR

Getting Involved with a TV Travel Show

As well as being asked what it's like to be on holiday all the time the other question people always want answered is: 'How did you get first get on telly?'

The answer is simple: 'The Travel Show' comes from BBC North in Manchester, I was a student at Manchester University and for the summer series in 1984 the producer decided to have a hitch-hiker on the programme. He interviewed me, I got the job and from that moment I was type-cast as a low-budget traveller.

The idea was that the hitch-hiker would only have £150 to live off all summer. Each week he would phone in a report to the main presenter and be given a target destination. Viewers would tune in to see how he was coping, how much money he had left and whether he had reached the new destination.

When I saw the job advertised I knew I could get it. I was 23, had hitch-hiked all over Europe and America, and had travelled literally hundreds of thousands of miles.

I met the producer and he explained the idea. Then I told him about all my previous hitch-hiking trips, said why I thought I was right for the job and added that if he used me he wouldn't have to worry about a thing — I already had such a wealth of travelling experience that I knew I could handle any situation that arose.

Until I was 18 I hadn't even flown on an aeroplane, which was ironic as I grew up very near to Heathrow Airport and had had so many different summer jobs there. Before I left school I'd been an airport driver, an aircraft cleaner and even an airline security man. But the job that I saw advertised, just after doing my A levels, seemed almost too good to be true.

It said: 'Overseas couriers wanted for airport-based freight company. Frequent travel. 18-25 years'. I phoned the company and they said they wanted messengers to deliver freight all over the world.

The work involved travelling on planes, delivering different packages – usually by taxi, and coming back in the evening at around 9 o'clock. Most of the destinations were in Europe and America, but occasionally they were further afield. Couriers worked four days a week and usually visited a different place each day.

The pay was £170 a month. I asked for an application form, went for an interview and started the following week.

For a hyper-active 18 year old it really was the most marvellous job in the world. Every day I'd fly to a different city. You could be sent anywhere – Paris, Rome, Brussels one day, Athens, Stockholm, Dublin the next. Sometimes you visited two or even three countries in one trip (although these understandably, weren't popular as you barely got out of the airports). I made at least six New York trips, went to Los Angeles, and once made a day-trip to Egypt. And every night, after flying in from some foreign part, I'd make my way home on my bike. It used to take me longer to cycle home to Sunbury-on-Thames than it did to get to Paris by plane.

After a couple of months I knew some of the people in the Heathrow office and could request where I wanted to go. My parents found this useful. Mum liked the fresh mozarella I got from Milan and would frequently say: 'Matthew, do try to get a Milan trip soon. That Italian mozarella is so much nicer than our local supermarket stuff.'

Dad did pretty well too: 'Matthew, I'm getting a bit low on those King Edward cigars. Could you do a New York trip and get me another box or two.' (They were eight times cheaper over there.) We could buy lots of duty-free each week, so as well as cigars, I kept my dad supplied with pipe tobacco, cigarettes and booze.

But despite all the different destinations, Germany was the country we went to most. I hated it at first – the people seemed to run around like robots and many cities were modern and ugly. But then I found that most young Germans were so keen to practise their English that it was incredibly easy to talk to them. I made friends all over Germany and had a girlfriend in Hamburg called Doris.

Whenever I got a Hamburg trip (we were told our destinations the evening before) I used to ring Doris with 10p pieces from a coinbox at the end of our road. 'Hey Doris, I'm coming to Hamburg tomorrow. I'm getting the 9 a.m. Lufthansa flight so I'll meet you by the lockers at the Haupt-bahnhoff at ten. Check with the airport if I'm late. See you tomorrow. Bye...'

She would then take the morning (or sometimes the whole day) off school. I'd arrive with 200 Marlboro – she was 16 and smoked like a chimney – and we'd do all my deliveries together.

Despite her name, Doris was a wild-child. She was intelligent, pretty and spoke excellent English. She also liked to drink and skive off school. But although Doris was great fun it was actually quite easy to meet girls anywhere.

First of all being young and English was always a novelty – we played on that like mad. The second reason was that we didn't care about talking to strangers – it didn't matter if we made fools of ourselves. We would probably never see them again. And the final reason was that we always had money. Every day we'd go out with £200-300 (and this was 1979) to cover our daily expenses.

We always carried big wads of cash as we needed it for so many things. When we arrived at an airport we often had to pay customs' duties; then we'd take taxis to do our deliveries – we could spend several hours in a taxi and the bill could come to over £100; then we needed money for international phone calls (we had to ring our London office every hour to see if they needed any collections in our city); and finally we needed money for our own personal allowances, as well as any emergencies.

The personal allowances were not great and these were one reason why couriers were young. No mature adult would have tolerated the £3 permitted for a lunch, or the £4 for an evening meal (especially in Switzerland or Sweden), and for trips that involved overnighting, no self-respecting businessman would have survived on the £6 hotel allowance. I often used to stay in youth hostels, although I did have several nights at stations, a couple at US army bases in Germany, and a night in a Milanese brothel (I ended up there when our Italian driver crashed his car and made me miss my flight. He couldn't find a reasonably priced hotel so he took me to a little place he knew. I didn't even realise it was a brothel until I went back to Milan and everyone said, 'Ciao Matteo, bordello man.')

But the allowances didn't bother me – most jobs for 18 year olds didn't pay any expenses and, as in those days I wasn't interested in food, I often saved money by taking packed lunches on trips. I'd go to Paris with a packet of cheese sandwiches, which my father found quite hilarious – 'You're going to the culinary centre of the world and you take your own cheddar cheese sandwiches!'

Despite the small allowances we always had cash in our pockets. When we met girls we could buy them drinks, cigarettes, snacks and take them on taxi tours of the cities. As most of the girls I knew were the same age or younger than me, and therefore still at school, they were sufficiently impressed. We could also bring our friends nice English presents – like the latest punk records, badges and T-shirts.

There was another reason I liked Germany, also to do with money. Every time we went to Germany we'd buy not just deutschmarks at Heathrow Airport but also a bag of 5ps.

'Going to Germany are you?' asked the bank clerks. That always gave me a shock — most of them knew that 5ps were the same size as deutschmarks and fitted many German coin-operated machines. It was such fun getting six times their value, that when I got to Germany I'd go crazy with monetary lust. I could never decide which machines to put them in (although most boys settled for Mars bars, condoms and peep-shows).

Another country that I enjoyed visiting was France. The company did two trips a day to Paris and I loved the 'Paris Overnight'. This involved taking a 5 o'clock evening flight to Paris, staying the night in our prepaid hotel (a seedy joint near the Bois de Boulogne), getting up next morning at seven and helping our Paris driver, André, to do the deliveries before returning to the airport at three.

I loved being able to practise my French; so André and I got on well from the minute we met, and after our first deliveries together we came to a great arrangement — I'd bring him duty-free scotch and he'd let me lie in while he did the deliveries himself.

That suited me as I adored Paris and already had a friend there. So André used to let me stay in bed and collected the packages without waking me. I'd then get up about nine or ten, visit a monument or meet my friend, and he'd pick me up near our office at three then take me back to the airport.

I used to try to get that trip (which also counted as two days' work) once a week if I could.

Although in some cities we just jumped in a taxi at the airport, at others we had to use public transport and make our own way into town. The deal on the Paris overnight trip was that we took the airport bus from Charles de Gaulle to the Air France terminal at Porte Maillot (just behind the Champs Elysées). Then we had a 40-francs allowance for a taxi to our little hotel.

As one of our main destinations, Paris always meant loads of deliveries and sometimes we'd have three sacks full of packages. But like most of the others, instead of taking a taxi at Porte Maillot, I preferred to cripple myself by dragging the sacks to the hotel, and keep the taxi allowance.

One night, when it was pouring with rain, I had a particularly cumbersome load — three sacks probably weighing 50-60 kilogrammes each. The hotel was about a mile away and I was simultaneously getting soaked and exhausted as I dragged them down the streets. I couldn't drag all three together so I'd do one, leave it on the pavement a few yards ahead, and then go back for the others.

I was rushing back to my sacks when suddenly two figures stepped out in front of me.

'*Bonsoir, Monsieur.*'

Oh no! I thought, I was going to get mugged.

'*Vous allez bien, Monsieur?*'

'*Oui, merci, très bien et vous?*'

Professional smiles looked me up and down.

'*Non, non ça va merci, je suis pressé, je vais à mon hotel.*' I declined their offer and said I was a courier taking my deliveries to my hotel. They then looked puzzled as I grabbed the two orange sacks and dragged them back down the pavement. Still looking perplexed, they retreated to their doorway.

Suddenly I had an idea. I looked back at the figures in the porch. They were bored and had no other clients. I ran back to their badly lit shelter.

I felt a bit stupid but made my proposal. '*Bonsoir*... I was just wondering whether you might be interested in... not... but ... whether it might be possible for you to... help me carry my bags. I'll pay you... you see I work as a kind of international postman, and I have a 40-franc allowance to take a taxi with my bags to the hotel. Normally I prefer to walk and spend the money but my bags are so heavy tonight, I think I've overdone it and now there are no taxis around. I know it might sound very cheeky but if you just help me pull these bags to my hotel − it's only a few hundred metres − I'll let you keep my allowance.' I immediately felt a fool and prayed that they wouldn't feel insulted.

They laughed. The bigger one shrugged her shoulders. '*Pourquoi pas?*' So I set off again helped by two giggling prostitutes. When we arrived at the hotel the old night porter could hardly believe his eyes. He must have seen a lot in his time − the hotel really was very seedy − but I'd arrived with, not just one, but two girls straight off the streets. Although these two weren't exactly girls.

Chloé and Dominique were 40 if they were a day, and both looked like classic theatrical French tarts. They had heavily made-up faces and both were wearing big coats, black stockings and high heels. *'Merci, merci beaucoup,'* I said, as we all dropped our sacks and got our breath back. I pulled out two 20-franc notes.

'Mais non, ça va... tu plaisantes, c'était marrant,' and first Chloé, then Dominique, shook their heads laughing and started to walk away.

'Wait, wait,' I said, 'Please, please let me thank you. Let me buy you a drink.' They laughed again. 'I really am grateful.'

They looked at each other and shrugged their shoulders. *'Pourquoi pas?'* said Chloé.

The night porter knew the drill with the sacks and pulled them behind his desk ready for André in the morning. I told him I wouldn't be long.

We had coffee and a chat in a nearby café. They didn't tell me much about themselves but both found my lifestyle amazing. They couldn't believe I went to a different country each day and kept saying how *incroyable* it was for a *bébé* to have such a job.

They did say that this street was where they usally worked and that they were there from Monday to Thursday. I asked them if they'd be there two days later and told them I'd also be back. Two days later, to my absolute delight, we didn't just meet up but they greeted me off the Air France airport bus. *'Bonsoir Mathieu, comment allez-vous? Vous avez des grands bagages ce soir?'*

The bus was full of businessmen and most looked completely astounded — I wasn't just being met by one but two laughing, joking Paris prostitutes. We went for another drink in our café.

Over the following four months I saw them at least five times. Chlóe and Dominique didn't meet me off the bus again but I'd occasionally see them as I was dragging my bags. They never talked much about their lives but always expressed great concern for me. Every time we met they asked, 'And how is the *bébé?*' And every time we parted they told the *bébé* to be careful. About a year after I'd stopped working as a courier I looked for them again but they'd gone.

One reason I thought working as a courier qualified me for the TV hitch-hiking role was because, apart from becoming streetwise (which was why I thought the producer wouldn't have to worry about me), each day was an initiative test. Most of us were teenagers

and we continually had to deal with foreign addresses on packages which turned out not to exist, foreign taxi drivers who tried to rip us off, and foreign customs men who, it seemed, sometimes unnecessarily delayed us (our couriers were convinced that in some destinations other companies had them paid off – we always seemed to take ages while other couriers zipped through in seconds).

Taxi drivers were the bane of our lives. We were pretty much at their mercy and sometimes they would really take advantage. One boy who didn't speak a word of German, once got in a taxi in Munich, threw all his packages onto the front seat and told the taxi driver to take him to the different addresses. One was a delivery in Stuttgart (for which he'd been told in the office to buy a rail ticket) but the taxi driver took him at his word and ended up driving him to Stuttgart. Despite his protestations he ended up paying a £200 bill and was sacked when he got back to London.

My biggest trials with taxi drivers were during my day trip to Egypt. I'd been warned about them by the other couriers and had been advised to pack a box of Quality Street. I was told to give some to the driver when I got in the car. After that, I was to use them as bargaining tools.

Driving through the boiling hot streets of Cairo I was soon sweating profusely. I'd ask the driver to put on the air-conditioning and he'd demand a ridiculous price. That's when I used the chocs. 'Would you like another Quality Street?' The price would immediately fall. When I asked him to put on some music, the whole thing happened again. 'Ten Egyptian pounds, effendi.' 'Would you like another green triangle?' 'Okay, for you effendi, five.'

Although the places we went to were fascinating, the things we delivered were generally boring – documents for multinational companies for instance. Occasionally, however, interesting things did crop up.

Once, I delivered a script and an air-ticket personally to Peter Sellers, who was at the Hotel de Crillon in Paris. I went through the revolving doors into the beautiful marbled lobby and saw him standing in front of me. He signed the receipt (and autographed a separate piece of paper) and gave me a 20-franc tip.

The weirdest thing I ever brought back was the prize-winning cauliflower from the Paris Agricultural Show. It weighed over 40 kilogrammes and was so enormous that it had to have its own seat on the plane. That was fun – I strapped it in and had all its drinks

and food. And when we got to Heathrow it was met by horticulturalists who sprayed it with water and whisked it off to a vegetable show.

The most ridiculous delivery I ever did was of something I collected in Los Angeles. I went to LA only once and I'd hardly arrived (I was zonked out in our airport office waiting for the driver to take me to the hotel) when a film studio rang.

They wanted a quote for an immediate delivery for a small package from LA to Madrid. We quoted the price via London (nearly everything went through our hub) and said it would take two days. That wasn't good enough. They wanted it to go there direct.

The girl in our office said that would be expensive. It wasn't on our schedule so we had to quote a 'special' which allowed for the airfare and expenses. 'A thousand dollars,' she said. 'Fine,' said the studios, 'send a car now.'

As I was the only courier available, I had to go straight off to the studios and then fly directly to Madrid. I picked up the package at reception. It was addressed to a famous Hollywood actor.

At the airport our agent did all the customs' work, then I went through to departures, carrying the package in my bag.

During the flight, I looked at the customs' manifest. 'One package containing two items of toiletry. Commercial value: $10.' My curiosity was really aroused. How could two bits of toiletry be worth $1,000 in freight costs?

Happily for me, customs opened the package at the other end. Inside were the items that this Hollywood star was paying $1000 to have personally delivered immediately, – a tube of cherry-flavoured toothpaste and a can of contraceptive foam.

It's a digression but there's a related follow up to this story. One of the things I occasionally do is public speaking and a couple of years ago, I was doing a speech for the annual convention of a big Conservative Ladies' Federation. I can't remember where it was – somewhere in northern England – but over 1,000 ladies were packed into a local civic hall.

I wasn't on until after lunch and all through the meal I'd been asking myself: 'Should I tell the courier story? Yes... No... Yes... No... Oh what-the-hell? I'll tell them.'

I was in full flow, everyone was attentive and then I came to the climax: 'So inside this package that this actor was paying $1,000 to have personally delivered from LA to Madrid was... a tube of cherry-flavoured toothpaste and a can of contraceptive foam...'

There was absolute silence. 'Oh no, I've blown it,' I thought, 'I'll never be invited again.' The silence seemed to last for ages. I smiled and 2,000 eyes stared disapprovingly through me.

Suddenly a little voice burst out from the back. It was an elderly lady who had to shout to make herself heard: 'What flavour was the contraceptive foam?' she squeaked. The silence was broken by laughter and the embarrassing situation was saved.

So they were my courier days and I told the producer about them when he interviewed me for 'The Travel Show' job.

CHAPTER FIVE

Hitch-hiking Around Europe on £150

I did my first 'Travel Show' on the day of my final exam. After an atrocious French history paper, and a quick drink in the university union, I rushed off to the BBC.

That evening, Paul Heiney, then presenter, gave me £150, live on the programme and told me to get to Italy in time for next week's show. I left the studio with my bags and was followed by a camera which broadcast me hitching on Oxford Road.

I stuck my thumb out for a few seconds and watched as the cars whizzed by. Then the credits rolled and it was back to the BBC for a drink.

I set off for real the following day but wasn't particularly in the mood for hitch-hiking round Europe for eight weeks on a budget of only £150. I'd wanted to celebrate the end of my exams and then have a relaxing break.

It wasn't even as if hitch-hiking was a great novelty. I'd done it loads of times since I was 18 and at the end of each trip I'd always sworn that next time I'd travel in style.

Little did I know that hitch-hiking for 'The Travel Show' would typecast me as a low-budget bum – the guy who went off to Spain with only 50 quid, who got stranded at airports with only £2, or who went off on buses to Athens. I'd much rather have been Alan Whicker.

The hitch-hiking assignment was harder than it would have been if I'd done it for pleasure. I'd get to one place, start settling in and make my weekly phone call to 'The Travel Show'. Paul Heiney would then give me my next destination and I'd have to pack my bags and set off. If I'd been doing it myself it would have been much slower paced and I'd have stayed in the places I liked.

My approach to surviving on the limited budget (it really was that small – I was £300 overdrawn by the end of the summer term so I didn't have anything extra) was to get jobs wherever I could; but not to expect payment in money. If I could just be given accommodation and food that would help me survive.

The only proper job I got was at Naples football stadium on the day the star Argentinian player, Diego Maradona, arrived; I sold some Maradona T-shirts and made an impressive £3.

But unpaid jobs weren't so hard to find. My favourite was on a camp-site near Siracusa in Sicily. First of all I booked in as an ordinary camper then asked the owner if he had any jobs I could do – I didn't want payment, just a free pitch on his site.

He was a lovely man, a doctor. His name was Paolo and his wife was called Celia. Whenever I tried getting jobs it was impossible to tell people that I was hitching for the BBC – that was so implausible, nobody would have believed me. (And when I didn't speak the language it was far too complicated to explain.) So my line was that I was in a student competition and that we all had to get round Europe and survive on a limited budget. I just about managed to convey this to Paolo, so he invited me to join him and Celia for dinner.

He had a man called Pino who looked after his site and Paolo said I could be his assistant. I therefore spent the next five days helping Pino do his least favourite jobs – like cleaning out the camp-site toilets. But it was still a great deal – not only could I pitch my tent free, but Paolo wouldn't charge me for many things in the camp-site shop. In addition I had several great meals with them.

From Sicily my instructions were to get to Malta – I was supposed to hitch a lift on a boat. And like most things on this trip, that was easier said than done.

Every day after cleaning out the toilets and picking up rubbish round the site I got the bus into town and then ran to the little pleasure port.

I didn't know anything about boats but I met people who spent their whole lives on them. Lots of the yachties had similar stories – they'd sold their houses (sometimes after taking early retirement) and spent the money on a boat. They then spent the year in sunshine – sailing to the Caribbean for winter and returning to the Med for summer.

All yachties are used to sail-bums hanging round ports for a lift. They were suspicious of me at first, especially as I had no experience, but after a couple of days I became a familiar figure to the British contingent and they'd tell me all about new arrivals – where they had come from and where they were off to.

Unfortunately no one was off to Malta. Several boats had come from the island, but they were all heading for other places. It was additionally unfortunate as I'd been told by 'The Travel Show' producer, to make sure I was in Malta by Thursday. A 'Travel Show' crew was there making a resort report and they wanted to capture me on film. The producer had told me to meet the crew by Queen Victoria's statue in Valletta on Thursday at noon.

What I didn't know was that Paul Heiney had told the programme's viewers that if they were having a holiday in Malta that week, they could meet me on Thursday.

When I couldn't get a lift I felt a real failure. I phoned the producer and told him I wasn't going to make it.

On Thursday British holiday-makers turned up at the statue. The film crew was there, but I was nowhere to be found. They waited until one, then two, then three and I still failed to arrive. Kathy Rochford was the resort report presenter. She did a piece on film, asking the question: 'Matthew, wherever have you got to?' That, along with an interview with some of the holidaymakers who hadn't been able to meet me, just added to the tension of the item. Nobody knew where I was and it really convinced people that the whole thing was real.

I was actually on my way to Dubrovnik. At the last minute I'd found a couple who'd said I could go there with them. I left the camp-site on Friday excited by the prospect of sailing and delighted that I'd save some more money.

Unfortunately, this trip had its own complications – the main one being the boat. *Dawn Lady* had been built in Exeter in 1923 (it said so on her hull). She'd obviously seen better days but her owner, Roy, was a pioneering chap (a strong, silent, macho type who worked half the year on Middle East oil wells) and liked to do his own thing.

Before we left he told me very proudly how he'd spent the whole winter in Malta putting up a new mast himself. As there hadn't been any wind between Sicily and Malta he hadn't been able to test it and had had to come over on the motor (not something sailors like doing as it uses up fuel and isn't proper sailing).

We were due to sail on Friday morning but there still wasn't any decent wind. He let me stay overnight on the boat and decided to wait until Saturday. Morning came and there was still no wind. We waited until afternoon then decided to leave anyway.

For two days we chugged over the calm Mediterranean using the Perkins engine (it was the same kind they fit on London taxis). I'd never sailed before and despite the calm sea, didn't particularly like it. I hated the smell of the exhaust, felt occasionally seasick, and my fragile stomach wasn't helped by the tepid water on board (there was no fridge) and the curries served up by his girl-friend. I also suffered a slight touch of sunstroke.

But there were some great bonuses. Frequently we'd be followed by groups of flying fish and once we even saw dolphins. And at night when I worked as the look-out (to make sure we didn't hit cruise ships – you'd see them going by in the distance) the stars and the sea were so beautiful I could just stare at them for hours.

On the third day the wind suddenly started to blow up some decent gusts. Roy got excited – at last he'd be able to test out his mast. We hoisted the sails and turned off the engine. 'This is what it's really all about, Matt,' he said proudly. 'This is proper sailing.'

Suddenly there was a terrible crack. The three of us looked up at the mast. Roy screamed: 'Get the sail down, get the bloody thing down.' The mast had a great split down its middle.

We began to drift, aimlessly floating on the sea. Roy looked as though he might burst into tears. His girl-friend tried to console him. I kept out of the way.

Not surprisingly things took a downward turn after that. The boat obviously wasn't going to make it to Dubrovnik, so Roy decided to pull into Otranto on the heel of Italy. It took a whole day to get there and he was in a bad mood for the rest of the trip. Not only had all his winter handiwork failed but he'd even had a witness to his failure. And that was after he'd boasted that he always did everything himself. He also had a pretty pathetic deck-hand.

By now I was eating practically nothing. I couldn't stand any more of his girl-friend's curries — she'd started serving them for breakfast and even the lukewarm water had a permanently spicy taste. He began to find fault with everything I did and none of us could wait to get back to land.

We limped into Otranto on the good old Perkins engine. They went to change some money and I ran off to the motorway.

When I phoned in to the programme I was told to head for the Alps and there was more drama as I hitched up Italy to the north.

CHAPTER SIX

Still Hitch-hiking – Things Get Worse

We were racing out of Naples when the driver suddenly pulled out a gun.

He pointed it straight at me, holding it in his left hand, while he held the steering-wheel in his right. The car was doing 120 kilometres an hour and his attention flickered between the windscreen and me. I swallowed. I was silent. I felt my bowels loosen. Suddenly he shrieked out with laughter.

'Imitazione! Imitazione!' He tossed the gun onto my lap and then slapped me on the shoulder. I was still numb with fear and his wild laughter burst out again.

It was indeed an imitation revolver – there were no holes in the barrel. I gave it back to him and he threw it into the glove compartment, chuckling and talking to himself.

As if that wasn't enough to dent my enthusiasm for hitch-hiking I soon found myself shaken up again. A few hours later I was in a badly air-conditioned Citröen belonging to a bald, fat, smelly, middle-aged salami salesman, who suddenly put his hand on my knee. He gave it a delicate squeeze and then a little stroke, so I screamed. Well, I didn't really scream but I snarled – every obscenity I knew. None were in Italian but he still got the message. He stopped the car and deposited me on the motorway.

Some people say bad things come in threes. So when a few minutes later two policemen told me they'd arrest me if I didn't get off the motorway immediately I wasn't over-surprised.

When I eventually reached Switzerland 12 hours later I headed for St Bernard's Monastery. This is where monks breed the big mountain-rescue dogs (the famous ones that rescue lost mountaineers, and have little brandy barrels round their necks). I'd read about it once as a kid in *Look and Learn* and thought it would be interesting to see. I also thought the monastery might lodge a poor, weary English traveller.

I was disillusioned when I arrived. The place was full of French and Swiss children, because it specialised in mountain holidays for schools. It also had a highly organised system for charging anyone who wasn't a school-kid if they wanted to stay at the monastery.

Luckily when I got to see one of the head monks he believed my story about being in a student travelling competition. He said I could stay free of charge if I helped out with some of the work.

The work turned out to be digging foundations for new kennels. So that was another good deal: in return for two mornings' digging I had two days' free board and lodging. I also got to feed the famous St Bernard mountain-rescue dogs.

'Get to St Tropez by Friday,' were Paul Heiney's instructions when I'd finished my Swiss phone report. A 'Travel Show' crew was there. And they wanted to film me too.

St Tropez was a dream. After surviving on an average of £3 a day I finally enjoyed several treats. The film crew took me out to restaurants and I stayed in a snazzy French hotel (albeit on the floor of the director's bedroom). They even took me out for a drink in a café where Charles Aznavour was sitting with some friends.

Unfortunately it all ended in less than two days. After finishing their resort report, the crew filmed me first on the beach, trying to sell ice-creams, then busking with a local magician (I spent three hours with him collecting his money – he gave me 25 francs). Then they drove me to the motorway and deposited me just east of Nice airport.

From France my destination was Portugal (I'm sure they only sent me there to make my studio route map look bigger) and after a nightmare journey through Spain (it really is the worst place to hitch-hike, my only decent lift was with a stoned Italian hippy who wanted me to drive while he smoked joints in the back with his girl-friend) I got as far as Oporto. I had two nights there in a suburb, staying with an Angolan family after I met the son on a bus. Then, with £25 left, it was time to start the long journey home.

It took three days to get to Calais and I managed to spend only £8. When I finally reached Dover I thought all my struggles would be over. I had this naive idea that having seen me on TV for the last eight weeks British drivers would be queueing up to take me. At the very least I thought, hitching would be easy.

Nothing could have been further from the truth. As all the cars rolled off the ferry they all then rolled past me. None of the returning holiday-makers had the slightest interest in picking up a hitch-hiker, so I walked to the start of the motorway where I thought I might stand a better chance.

Things were no better there. One hour passed, then two, then three and still I hadn't had a single lift. I'd done 6,000 miles all over Europe and I couldn't even get out of Dover.

Finally a very old and battered Mark 2 Cortina stopped. 'Jump in,' said the driver. 'I'm only going a few miles down the road...'

As it turned out he'd done a bit of hitching himself. 'France, Spain, even went to Morocco once.' We talked about the joys and the perils of it all. I told him about the Italian with the gun and about the salami salesman who'd put his hand on my knee.

All the time on my trip I'd stupidly been without sun-glasses. It was now 3 o'clock and the unusually strong English sun was beaming directly through the windscreen. I pulled down the sun-flap.

Two dozen condoms fell onto my lap.

'Oh well,' said the driver, after an embarrassing silence. 'At least you know I'M not a poofter...'

He dropped me off 10 minutes later.

I arrived back in Manchester after help from the Greater Manchester Police. They stopped because I was illegally hitching on the motorway (after being deposited by one driver on the hard shoulder) but instead of arresting me they offered a lift.

'I've seen you,' said one of the policemen. 'You're the one who's been going all round Europe with no money. Yeah, I saw you last week – you were in Portugal.' They switched on the blue light and I finished my journey in style. We raced up the M6 then they dropped me off on Oxford Road in Manchester, at the front door of BBC North.

PART THREE

The Special Assignment

CHAPTER SEVEN

Early Trips and 'Travel Show' Viewers

My next 'Travel Show' series was the following summer. I don't know who came up with the special assignment but I thought the idea was brilliant. Each week I was to be given a mission — go anywhere, do anything — without ever having a clue what it was. Every assignment was to be a total surprise, only to be revealed live on the programme.

Many viewers frequently used to ask me if the trips really were a surprise each week. The answer is most definitely yes. The producer used to go to the most ridiculous lengths to hide them from me. False lines would be put in the printed scripts and a dummy assignment inserted on to the autocue for rehearsal. When it came to the broadcast programme, which used to be transmitted 'live', the dummy assignment was then taken out and replaced by the real thing. One week however, with a new autocue girl, this caused a major mistake.

The autocue person has the script on a scroll which is projected on to the camera. The presenter looks at camera, sees the autocue and reads it, while giving the impression that he or she is talking directly to the viewer. The autocue person's job is to scroll through the script precisely in time with the presenter. On this occasion we did the rehearsal and Penny Junor told me I was going to Romania. 'Apparently,' she said, 'due to local electricity shortages there's an evening curfew operating in Romanian holiday resorts. British tourists have given us reports of power being switched off in the early evening. Your assignment Matthew, is to go to Romania and to see what it's like having a holiday where night-life ends at eight in the evening.'

But this was only the dummy. The real assignment was put in at eight fifty-five just before the programme went out live. At nine twenty-eight Penny read it out and told me I was going to Spain, on some typical low-budget challenge. Then she turned to the camera to read out the next item but found to her horror it wasn't there. Instead the script said that Matthew was off to Romania — the autocue girl had forgotten to remove the dummy trip. It seemed like forever until she finally realised what had happened. She scrolled through Romania and landed half-way through the next story. Penny was completely confused and while the autocue script was spun back and forth she hardly knew what to say. There was silence in the studio. It was only for seconds but felt like eternity. Luckily normal service soon resumed. The autocue girl found the next item, Penny read it out and quickly said goodbye before she ran out of time. Needless to say it caused much debate in the programme office next day, but at least it proved the measures the producer took to make the trips a total surprise.

My first travel assignment was a very simple one — going to Malaga on a 'flight only' deal and finding my own accommodation. There were so many cheap 'flight only' tickets being offered that I had to see whether such a proposition was practical for an ordinary holiday-maker.

I found a room easily but it was in a small *hostal* not a major tourist hotel. A room for four nights in one of the bigger places would have cost more than the price of a full week's holiday bought in Britain. It made me realise that package deals to major tourist destinations are often better value than trips put together independently — the tour operators have such great purchasing power that they can buy up rooms at prices much lower than individuals can usually negotiate. In Torremolinos I met a Glaswegian family — a couple and two kids — wandering round the town with their suitcases. Their flights had cost them £50 each but hotels were quoting £80 a night — almost half their holiday budget.

A couple of weeks later I was given a 'flight only' ticket to Corfu. Things were more practical here. Holiday accommodation was, and still is, usually family-owned on Greek islands and is therefore on a much smaller scale. There were people at the airport offering rooms to rent and in many of the resorts you would see 'accommodation available' signs in houses. Finding a room was so easy that I have rarely bothered pre-booking Greek island accommodation since then. At most of the ports and airports, incoming tourists are greeted by locals offering rooms and usually you can be settled within a few minutes of arriving.

As the series progressed the assignments became more adventurous. I was sent to Venice where, in an attempt to control the numbers of tourists, the authorities had recently introduced policies discriminating against low-budget travellers. I, of course, was given very little money – £50 for the week. I found that it had become illegal for anyone to eat snacks in St Mark's Square – unless they were sitting in a café. I took a sandwich out of my rucksack and found myself being moved on by police. When dusk fell I didn't have money for a hotel so I went to spend the night at the station. Plenty of young budget travellers were already settled there. I got into my sleeping-bag but half-way through the night the police came to hose the station down. They said they only wanted to clean the floor but it was a convenient way of waking us abruptly and forcing us all to leave the station.

On another assignment I had to spend the weekend on six different cross-channel ferries to come up with tips for ferry travellers (I found that the kindergarten was the least crowded part of the boats so while other passengers fought for seats, I had a relaxed crossing with the few mums and toddlers who'd discovered it).

On a different occasion I was sent to Majorca with only £50 to see if I could reach the island under my own steam (that meant hitch-hiking) for less than the cost of a bargain return flight (we had one on the programme for £55). I failed miserably. I hitched down to Barcelona for less than £30 but then could not get any further. And on another trip I was sent to the Austrian Alps and told to be a vegetarian for a week.

This wasn't easy in Mayerhofen where I found restaurants offering starters like 'Scrambled eggs and brains' and main courses like 'Sliced heart and lungs'. But I did find that local tourist offices had handy lists of places that could cater specifically for vegetarians.

Innsbruck, however, was a joy. I found the most wonderful vegetarian restaurant, the 'Philippine Vegetarische Kuche', on Mullerstrasse (near the post office). The meatless schnitzel and the Erdbeeren Grossmutterart (sauce-dipped strawberries) were delicious so if ever you're in Innsbruck I can thoroughly recommend it.

As the assignment idea progressed the trips became more and more challenging. The producer came up with increasingly testing ideas and this was how I found myself staying in the nudist camp, having my leg put in plaster and spending six days on a coach.

There was however, one advantage in being the fall-guy for a TV producer's mad schemes – I had the sympathy of many 'Travel Show' viewers. Most TV presenters who work on holiday programmes find themselves having to justify being on holiday all the time. Of course, they are working but viewers often find this hard to appreciate. I'm frequently called a 'lucky chap' now but in the old days many people would say that they certainly did NOT fancy my job. On one occasion such public sympathy helped enormously.

'This week,' said Penny, 'you're off to Ibiza and Majorca. But I'm afraid you're not going to be seeing much of the islands because, as you know, long aircraft delays have been causing problems this summer – and we want you to experience them firsthand.

'When you arrive at Majorca airport you'll go straight to the departure lounge. You're going to be there for 24 hours, in the position of someone waiting for his aircraft. When your 24 hours are up, you fly to Ibiza and on arrival you also go to the departure lounge. You spend another 24 hours in that one and experience another long delay. You won't be able to leave the departure lounges – your movements will be strictly monitored – and because most people have spent all their money by the end of their holiday, you will only have £4 for this trip. That's £2 for Majorca and £2 to spend in Ibiza. We want you to come back with tips for travellers who find that their aeroplane's delayed when they have hardly any money left. Good luck. Come back and tell us all about it next week.'

The assignment was another potentially awful one but luckily it turned out to be not quite so bad. The security men at Palma airport were expecting me. They'd been told to let me into the departure lounge but not to let me out for 24 hours.

Inside it was like a refugee camp. Numerous planes had been delayed and hundreds of passengers were sprawled everywhere. After four hours in a corner on the floor with well-read copies of all the English papers that I'd collected off my incoming charter flight, I went to the bar for a Coke. I'd hardly started sipping when the departure lounge filled up with even more people. They were British and many carried Gatwick Airport 'See Buy Fly' bags.

A woman suddenly spotted me and shouted: 'Look, look – it's Matthew Collins, the one they send all over the place. Matthew – you poor boy! Is this your assignment? We saw him on the programme just today – he's got to spend 24 hours in two different airports to see what it's like experiencing a big aircraft delay. And they've only given him £4. They don't treat you very well, do they, dear? How long have you been here? Would you like a bite to eat? We're on our way to Menorca – the plane couldn't land because of bad weather so we've been diverted to Palma for a while. Oh my – fancy seeing you here... we only saw you on 'The Travel Show' a few hours ago...'

Two hundred other passengers were on the same flight. 'So it's not a con then?' said a bricklayer from Peckham. 'You do do it for real? And you really will spend all that time here?' He looked amazed and bought me a drink.

Soon I was being offered things by other passengers on the flight. They tutted and said what a sadist the producer must be. They remembered my leg-in-plaster trip and asked me about previous assignments. As well as drinks and food many gave me money and when the departure of the Menorca flight was finally announced, and everyone rushed in a panic towards the gate, dozens of people threw me coins or pressed change into my hand. It was 1 a.m. before I was alone again. I counted the money – I had £4 and 1,200 pesetas.

The lounge was still packed with people. I couldn't find a seat but after wandering around for 20 minutes I discovered the maternity room – it was even more tranquil than the ferry's kindergarten. It was also dark and empty. There were plenty of cots but also lots of seats. I shut the door, fell asleep and didn't wake up until 8.30 a.m. when a group of Spanish cleaners came in and started laughing, thinking I'd missed my flight home.

Ibiza Airport was worse than Palma – this time there were no diverted British tourists to help me. Another problem was the airport's location near a sand-flat so mosquitoes were always buzzing around. Many of the departing British passengers had arrived at the airport in their holiday wear – shorts, T-shirts and trainers – and were regretting it, not just because the cool air-conditioning made them cold after several hours' waiting, but also because they were so vulnerable to mosquito bites. Those wearing perfume and aftershave found themselves bitten even more – apparently mosquitoes are attracted to the smell – so I was glad that I had a jumper in my duffle bag and extra pleased I wasn't wearing Brut.

A few weeks later however, when I was cycling through France, viewers played a part in my assignment again. This challenge had been to cycle along the famous Route Napoleon (the road that runs from Grenoble to Cannes) in less than four days. Despite the time factor it had all the promise of a very pleasant trip.

I collected my bicycle at Grenoble station, which had been arranged through the SNCF, French Railways (they have a great system — you can hire a bicycle from over 50 different stations in France), and set off on my way with a map. Unfortunately much of the Route Napoleon went along a main road, and as I foolishly kept strictly to the most direct way at the beginning (along the National 85 — to save the little precious time I had), I had fast cars and lorries hurtling past me continually. When I did make small detours — branching off on to the D roads then the smaller mountain lanes — the atmosphere changed completely. Butterflies danced on my handlebars and the only road blocks consisted of sheep, but it was exhausting cycling up to 1,500 metres carrying a rucksack and two panniers.

One day, feeling lazy after six hours' hard cycling, I got off my bike, turned it upside down (so it would look broken) and stuck out my thumb to try to hitch.

I'd expected the French, who are mad keen on cycling, to pity a poor cyclist in distress but I hadn't been prepared for the speed with which my first lift arrived. I had had my thumb out for just a few seconds when a pick-up truck came to a halt. 'C'est quoi le problème?' asked the driver. 'Gears,' I shouted, 'les vitesses. They're jammed — bloquées.' He offered me a lift all the way to Cannes and told me to throw my bike in the back. He dropped me off at the railway station where the Chef de Gare was waiting to greet me. He rang up the local newspaper Nice Matin who promptly arrived to do a picture story about this 'courageous BBC reporter' who had cycled all the way from Grenoble to Cannes, and took me out for a delicious slap-up lunch.

Unfortunately some English holiday-makers whom I'd met in a café earlier on my trip had seen me getting a lift. They had taken photos of me getting into the truck (and putting my bike on board) and then sent the film to 'The Travel Show'. That was a great reward for talking to them all about the programme. The producer got the film, had it developed and then gave me a ticking-off about not playing by the rules and deceiving him.

CHAPTER EIGHT

The Undercover Timeshare Investigation

It wasn't long however, before I was back in Spain. This time my mission was to 'get a girl-friend'.

'Nice one,' I thought. Then I learnt that I was going to the Costa del Sol to investigate timeshare. The programme had received sacks of letters from viewers complaining about irritating touts. It seemed that British couples in the area were being constantly pestered to visit new timeshare developments. Touts promised anything to get them to the sites and once they were there, the tourists, who'd been told they were 'under no obligation', were subjected to high-pressure sales spiel.

Some had cracked and signed. One of our viewers had found to his horror, that he'd promised to pay thousands of pounds for two weeks in an apartment in November.

My brief was to vist a development to see what the sales pitch was like and to come up with tips for tourists to avoid being pestered. First of all however, to make sure I was approached, I had to find myself a girl-friend (it turned out they only solicited couples because they thought they were more likely to buy).

There was one other feature of the trip. So that I wouldn't be spotted as a spy (and to make things more interesting for 'Travel Show' viewers, as well as give the producer a thrill) I was to be in disguise. At the end of the programme I went into make-up and collected a moustache, glasses and a hat.

A few hours later I was in Malaga. I took the train from the airport to Fuengirola, and checked into a small Costa del Sol hotel. I'd headed for Fuengirola because I knew that the bus garage was a favourite haunt for local British timeshare touts.

I dumped my case and went to find some supper. Although there are signs all over the Costa del Sol advertising things like 'Real English Food', 'Tea like Mother Makes' and 'Val's Special Steak-And-Kidney Pie' there are places where you can still be served good Spanish food (after all the locals have to eat somewhere). I went into a tapas bar and, as I ordered a coffee, noticed a small poster on the wall, advertising a vegetarian restaurant. (Spain is surprisingly good for vegetarian restaurants - there are increasing numbers of them in big towns and cities, and the dishes are often based exclusively on wonderful, fresh, local produce instead of rice, pasta and pulses as in Britain.) This one promised *'deliciosos legumbres frescos'* − delicious fresh vegetables − with *'muchas especialidades exoticas'* − lots of exotic specialities. I decided to give it a try.

I was shown to my table by a brown-haired girl, who didn't look Spanish, wearing a black swishing skirt. I ordered a beer and decided on the avocado soup with the stuffed aubergine from the cheap 600 pesetas menu. The food more than exceeded all my expectations so I told the waitress how much I'd enjoyed it.

It turned out she was Danish, from Århus in Jutland and was spending a year learning Spanish. Her name was Ulla-Birgitte. She'd been on the Costa del Sol for two months, but had only worked in the restaurant for three days. 'What were you doing before?' I asked.

'Oh − a very stupid thing,' she said. 'I worked for a company selling timeshare.'

'PERFECT!' I thought. 'She can give me inside information and might even agree to be my girl-friend.'

I told her excitedly what I was doing and once she'd finished serving she told me about her previous job. She said she'd arrived in Torremolinos from Grenada with very little money and had met some Swedish boys in a bar who'd boasted that they earned 100,000 pesetas (£500) a week by packing tourists off to timeshare complexes. All they had to do was get them in a taxi. They received commission for every one that went to the developments; and if the tourists signed up to buy they could make up to a million pesetas more.

The Swedes made it sound so easy that she'd decided to give it a try. She went for an interview at the company headquarters (they rented an office in a smart hotel) and was instantly offered a job, but before she was allowed on the streets, she first had to do a quick sales course.

On the course she learnt how to approach tourists (she was only allowed to approach Scandinavian ones – the British did Brits, the Germans did Germans). She learnt what to say to them; how to say it; how to reassure them (she was never allowed to use the word 'timeshare'); and even how to hold herself in front of the tourists when standing and making her pitch. She had a book filled with course notes which she promised to show me.

I still couldn't believe my great luck – I'd only been in Malaga a few hours and already had half a story.

When I told her that I wanted to visit a complex, and that I needed a partner so the touts would invite me, she thought the idea sounded fun and agreed to meet up next day. She wasn't worried about accompanying me in Fuengirola because she'd worked further down the coast.

The only problem we envisaged was that she didn't look British. If she was to be my girl-friend, it would be better if she looked more English.

The next day I met her outside the vegetarian restaurant. She was wearing white stilettos and a tight, red, shiny skirt but instead of resembling a Tracey from Basildon she looked like a Copenhagen porn star. In contrast I was sporting a furry moustache, a white British sun-hat, and a pair of old horn- rimmed dark glasses. I looked like some ancient colonial character who thought he was still part of the Raj.

'We don't exactly make a natural couple,' I said. 'People will think I've hired you for the day... Never mind – let's give it a try.'

We walked towards the bus garage (the touts all worked there because it was right in the centre of town and they were able to catch plenty of tourists about to get on or off buses) and waited for the sharks to approach us.

There was a large collection of shifty characters already on parade with their clip-boards. 'Excuse me – are you British?' they'd say, to sunburnt couples wearing trainers, shorts and T-shirts, who couldn't possibly have been anything else. 'Are you on holiday here?' It was obvious they weren't here on business. 'Are you having a good time in Fuengirola?' Most of them looked deadly serious.

The couples usually tried not to react by keeping a completely straight face and continuing to walk briskly, as the smiling touts pursued them with their patter.

We circled the bus garage twice. Nobody bothered to approach us.

'You think I should change my clothes?' asked Birgitte.

'No — it's my fault,' I said. 'I look so ridiculous, I probably frighten them all off.' I put on different glasses and we returned to the bus bays to see if we could tempt any to pester us.

This was our third attempt and some of them seemed to eye us suspiciously but suddenly one leapt out with his clip-board. 'Excuse me, are you British?'

I nodded.

'Are you on holiday here?'

I nodded.

'Are you having a nice time in Fuengirola?'

I smiled.

'Can I just ask you if you're married?'

I frowned and looked at Birgitte.

'Engaged?'

I nodded a timid 'yes'.

'Do you like water-parks?'

I mused as if to say 'maybe'.

'How about brandy then? I bet you like that. Or what about champagne?'

I beamed, to say 'yes definitely'.

'Well,' he went on. 'If you're interested in a tour of a beautiful new development park — it really is lovely, I can assure you — and listen to one of our presentations — they won't take up much of your time I promise — and just jump in a taxi right now — you won't have to pay, we'll see to that — I'm telling you that in 15 minutes time, you'll have your hands on any free gift of your choice. It could be some brandy, a bottle of champagne or a free ticket to one of Spain's biggest aquaparks.'

I glanced at Birgitte, she glanced at me, and both of us looked at him open-mouthed. 'Does that sound like an interesting proposition?' he asked. I smiled at him naively and looked back at Birgitte.

'Well,' he said (I could see him thinking 'these two are a right pair of plonkers'), 'if you just pop into this taxi and take this piece of paper and show it to the office when you get there − you'll get your gifts, I guarantee it.' He opened the taxi door and we climbed in, a couple of lambs to the slaughter.

The development was up in the hills and on our way there Birgitte and I worked out our story. 'Right,' I said, 'We've been going out for two years, okay? We live together in London. I'm a civil servant and you're a secretary at the Danish Embassy. My name's Michael Williams and yours is Beatrix Hanson. It's no use us both being British − it won't work. Oh yes − we own our flat. We've got a mortgage together. Let's make them think we've got some money.'

We arrived at a barrier in front of an office. The taxi deposited us, collected a 1,000 peseta note from a girl through a window, and steamed off back south to Fuengirola.

'Good morning,' said the girl. 'Come on in. Would you like tea or coffee?' The office was like a doctor's waiting room, filled with several other nervous couples. The girl took our paper, asked us our names and made notes. A team of men marched in. Different names were called including, soon, 'Mr Williams and Miss Hanson...'

'My name's Bryan,' said a man rushing up to us. He shook our hands vigorously and motioned us out of the office. He was a small chap, unshaven, with unpolished brown shoes, a dirty white shirt, and very creased dark linen trousers. A packet of Benson and Hedges was wedged in his breast pocket and a fag was sticking out of his mouth. 'So, are you having a nice time here?' he asked. 'Gorgeous, isn't it?' He took in a deep breath and grinned. 'Ab-sol-ute-ly, blin-king gor-geous.' He spoke with a Manchester accent.

'So have you been to Spain before?'

('Only about five hundred times,' I thought.) 'No,' I said. 'Never.'

'And what about you, Beatrix?' She shook her head. 'It is Beatrix isn't it?' He looked at a piece of paper. 'Yes − Beatrix Hanson. So what do you do then, Beatrix?' He led us out of the office and onto a lawn in the middle of a collection of dinky Andalusian-style houses.

'I'm a secretary,' said Birgitte.

'That's interesting,' he said. 'I bet you look forward to your holidays...'

'Oh yes, very much,' replied Birgitte obligingly.

He gave us a quick tour of the complex. 'Isn't it just gorrrr-geous?' he kept saying. He pointed to a pond. 'Beautiful lake,' he said, 'Stocked with fish. Do you like fishing, Michael? They're soon going to fill it with perch.'

I nodded in approval. We walked onto another rolling lawn.

'And this,' he said, 'is going to be a golf course. Fifteen holes. Are you a golfer, Michael?' I shrugged my shoulders gently as if to say maybe, some day.

'Right, over there's the swimming pool. Half the official Olympic size. Not bad, eh Mike? And I suppose you like your swimming too, Beatrix.' Birgitte nodded again obligingly.

'So how does the idea of staying here grab you? Because you could, you know... and I'm not just talking about once. You could come here IN PERPETUITY. Imagine that, eh? IN PERPETUITY...' He gave us some time to let the concept sink in. I touched my moustache – it was starting to come unstuck. My glasses had steamed up and the hat had made my head feel all sweaty.

After a visit to the show-flat (where the gold-plated bath taps, white furniture, 26-inch colour TV and mirrors on the master bedroom ceiling were all admired – in between claims of, 'And this could all be yours – IN PERPETUITY – imagine!') he asked me if I liked the idea of coming to this GORGEOUS part of Spain and staying here – IN PERPETUITY – for the rest of my natural life. 'And do you plan children?' he asked nosily. 'Because you can bequeath it to them so they too can enjoy it – IN PERPETUITY themselves. Right let's just go over and discuss a few things.' He led us to a small office opposite the one we'd arrived at.

'Okay – what did you say you did, Mike? A civil servant? How much do you make in a year?'

I mumbled a figure. 'Fifteen grand.'

'What about you then, Beatrix?'

'Excuse me?' Birgitte said.

'What about you, love? How much are you on a year?'

'I'm sorry?'

'Salary, dear. What did you say were – a touch-typist?'

'A Dutch typist?... No, I am Danish.'

'Yes, I know you're Danish, love, but you said you were a shorthand typist.'

'Short... hands?'

'Look, love — what are you on?'

'On?'

'Ten,' I interjected.

'Ten grand... right — plus your whack, Mike... that puts you on a joint income of 25 grand a year. Not a bad little screw is it? Could be worse. Now you've got a mortgage. How much is that for?'

'Look, I'm not sure I want to answer that question,' I said.

'All right then,' he went on. 'What sort of outgoings do you have on your flat every week.'

'I don't know — 200 quid a week between us, with bills and everything,' I said.

'Right,' he continued, doing a few calculations on some paper. 'Now you spend over £10,000 a year just on your little flat in London. I suppose it's a bit poky is it? What area is it in?'

'Er... Clapham,' I replied.

'Not exactly upmarket is it, Clapham? Well imagine... you spend all that money just to survive in London... Now I know you've got to live there 'cause your work's in the city — but listen to this... You've seen everything that's here and you like it, don't you? Yes, you do Beatrix — I've seen it in your eyes. And you Mike — yes I know you do too. Now you both work hard and you deserve a bit of luxury, so what would you say if I told you that you could have your own little place here — your own piece of paradise, IN PERPETUITY — for less than eighteen hundred quid? What do you say about that then eh?..'

He fixed a cold stare on Birgitte. 'Er... marvellous,' she said.

'What about you then, old mate?'

'Great,' I said.

'So let's do it then. You've got a credit card?' and he pulled out of a drawer, like a magician conjuring up rabbits, a series of forms for us to sign.

'Remember — IN PERPETUITY... Now just stick your name on those two lines there, sign this slip... and this will be yours forever.'

At that moment, with the hat making my head sweatier than

ever, my moustache becoming rapidly unstuck, and the salesman staring intensely right through me, I suddenly felt worried that I really would sign on the dotted line, just like some of the poor people who'd written to us, and end up with a week's share of something I certainly didn't think was paradise, for the rest of my natural born days.

'Hang on,' I said, coming to my senses. 'What about service charges? You haven't even talked about them.'

'Right, well, I'm glad you mentioned servicing, because we have here, right at our disposal, one of the best property management companies in Spain. Obviously there's a modest annual charge – for maintenance, administration, insurance, etc. but I can assure you that it's a lot less than for any other developments around here... Looking at what you're buying – a Stage One Starter Studio – the charges will be... £450 a year...'

'No, I'm sorry, I'm not interested,' I said decisively. 'We want to leave, if you don't mind.'

'Come on, come on, Mike – be reasonable. Think about it – you're getting your own piece of paradise in perpetuity and all you have to do is sign here now.'

'I'm sorry, I'm really not interested.'

'Look – maybe we could work out a discount.' He did a few more quick calculations. 'Seventeen hundred quid – because you're one of my first couples on the site.'

'No, I'm sorry.'

'Sixteen hundred quid, if you sign here today and pay seventy-five quid up front.'

'I'm sorry, no.'

'Sixteen hundred quid and you're turning me down. Mike, I can't believe you're doing this to me. Come on pal – after all the trouble we've been to today. All the things I've shown you. All the things we've talked about.'

'No,' I said firmly. 'We're really not interested.'

'Really not?'

'No.'

'Definitely?'

'No.'

'All right then mate – it's your personal choice.' And he got up, lit a fag and left the office.

We crossed the little road and asked the girl in the other office (where still more couples were waiting to be offered bits of paradise) whether we could get a taxi back to Fuengirola. She said she'd call us one. 'And what about our free gift?' I asked.

'What do you want?'

'A bottle of champagne please.' She handed me some cheap sparkling wine.

Our taxi was just pulling up when suddenly there was a potentially volatile situation. A lady waiting in the office to be shown the site with her husband, rushed out and approached us. She looked me up and down, stared me in the eyes, and announced with quiet triumph and joy: 'It's you, isn't it? I knew it was. You can't hide from us with that disguise. We knew it was you – we watch you every week. You're on your timeshare investigation aren't you? Got your girl-friend then? And your free bottle of champers? How's it going with the timeshare?.. All right?..'

She rushed into the office to get her husband. 'John, John,' she shouted, 'It IS him – I knew it was. It's Matthew doing his timeshare investigation. Get the camera quick. Hey, John, come here...' But I didn't wait for John. I pushed Birgitte into the taxi, scrambled onto the back seat myself and gave the driver orders to get away as quickly as possible. With the smell of burning rubber on the hot Spanish tarmac, we turned around and screeched towards Fuengirola.

Back in town Birgitte showed me her book of notes taken from her timeshare selling course. We reproduced part of it on the programme. Later, in a bar I met other British timeshare touts – some of whom boasted that having been unemployed at home they now earned great wages here. Obviously I never told any of them what I was doing – instead I said I wanted to stay in Spain (the classic route into timeshare selling was for people to come on holiday and then not want to go home) and a couple of them told me where I might find a job.

Perhaps stupidly, I went for an interview. A woman asked me what I did in England. I said I'd been a hairdresser (it was the first thing that came into my head) and that I'd got fed up with it and wanted something different. She asked me if I liked a challenge. I said of course. She also asked me if I liked money. I said definitely. Then she gave me a clip-board, said I could earn over £600 a week just by talking to tourists, and that all I had to do was to ask them to visit a high-class new set of apartments. Everything was legit she said. The apartments were beautiful and it wasn't timeshare. I was paid on commission and earned more if my clients bought a property. Unlike Birgitte's company, this one didn't insist I attended a sales course first and I was sent out directly on the streets.

I did it for a few minutes to see what it was like and, after the few people I'd accosted had treated me like a scourge to be avoided at all costs, was very glad to give up. Imposing myself full time on unwilling people when all they wanted was a holiday in peace, I would have found soul-destroying. But one man, clearly not interested in timeshare, told me where to buy the very best timeshare-tout deterrent. It was a T-shirt with the words (printed in extremely bold letters): 'YES I AM BRITISH, YES I AM ON HOLIDAY, YES I AM MARRIED, BUT NO I DO NOT WANT A TIMESHARE – SO PLEASE KINDLY **** OFF!' They were sold at the midnight café at Benalmadena Mar. I bought one and showed it on the programme.

CHAPTER NINE

British Lager Louts

During the 1980s I made many trips to Spanish Mediterranean resorts. One of the most memorable was to San Antonio in Ibiza, where I was told to find a job as a 'prop'.

A 'prop's' job is to entice holiday-makers into a bar or nightclub – he or she stands at the entrance and 'propositions' all passers-by. I had to see how easy it was to work as one and to try to discover all their secrets.

San Antonio is a brash tourist resort. In the late 1980s many of the young British who went there had a reputation for noise and drunkenness. There were so many bars, lots of them British-owned, that competiton for clients was fierce. That was where the 'prop's' job came in.

Although my brief on the programme had been to work as a prop, once we had gone off air the producer told me he was interested in this mainly as a lead into an investigation of the problems of youth drinking. The British tabloids had been making so much fuss about lager louts that he wanted to know if young Brits really were appallingly behaved or whether the fuss was just hype.

It wasn't hard to find a job – the work was so poorly paid that there was always a high turnover of staff (some made as little as £3 a night) and after trudging round a few bars on the day I arrived, I was told I could start later that night.

Many of the 'props' used different kinds of attention-seeking gimmicks and I was offered a sign with an arrow which I very obviously pointed to my bar. Some boys used more direct methods but the secret of success was always the same: GET THE GIRLS IN. If you got the girls in, the boys would inevitably follow. Some lads relied on their charm – a smile, a wink, a kiss, a few flattering words – while others literally picked up the girls and carried them into their bar. Once they'd got a few women in they could make promises to all the passing chaps: 'All right you lot? It's packed out with women in here – you want to get lucky tonight? This is definitely your place.' Other lures were less subtle: 'Come on lads – guaranteed bonks and best value beer in Ibiza.' In addition to the promises of available sex, many bars also sold cheap booze. If you arrived before a certain time you could enjoy all the happy hour specials – two drinks or measures for the price of one – and even if you started in the middle of the evening the beer would usually cost less than at your local at home.

With such a cocktail of promises, the potential for trouble was enormous. The most obvious cause was when one of the promises went unfulfilled. Most lads usually got the cheap booze but not all ended up with a girl (particularly aggravating when the 'prop' who had enticed them all in had probably boasted that he 'had' six different 'birds' a week). In such cases the boys would then go on drinking until:

1) They went home
2) They passed out
3) They got arrested by the police

At the time I was there, number three was quite a popular option.

I decided to visit the local police station to see if the British boys really were the problem, as our tabloid papers all said they were, or whether other nationalities were guilty of drunken misbehaviour as well. To my surprise a senior policeman agreed to see me. He told me that local people had become so disgusted with certain types of young foreign tourist that they had introduced a new policy of locking up for the night anyone who was drunk and causing trouble. They had had so many cases of fights, vandalism and generally anti-social behaviour that they had decided something had to be done. 'And are the British boys the biggest cause of trouble?' I asked.

'My friend,' he said. 'Why don't you come here at three in the morning and see how many of your compatriots we've locked up?'

After a night working as a prop in the West End area of San Antonio I could see the potential for arrests. The narrow streets were swarming with young people, the bars were packed out, lads urinated openly in the streets and others puked-up quite freely, encouraged by their mates to vomit more.

At two-thirty in the morning, when most of the bars were still swinging, I traipsed back to the police station and was presented to a colleague of the officer I had met earlier. He said they had had a quiet night.

'Not too bad — 18 arrests.'

'How many of them British?'

'I don't know.'

He led me down to the cells. There were over 20 of them and nearly all were full of young British men. They weren't really men but boys. The average age was 18 — some were younger but few had reached their early twenties. As far as I could understand, they had been arrested on charges ranging from disturbing the peace to smashing up property. The aim of the arrest policy, the officer said, was to scare them into not behaving anti-socially again, but looking at these lads I had my doubts it was working. Nearly all had anger written on their faces. They knocked on their cell bars, swore at the policemen and some even spat in contempt. A comotose Swede lay on his floor, and a drunk Brit burbled some songs. But the rest looked ready for war. I walked round the cells, talking to the inmates, feeling a little like Prince Charles. 'So what are you in for?' I asked one.

He spat out a stream of rambling obscenities concluding with a promise to take his revenge the moment he got out of his cell. I asked another boy the same question. He said some Germans had picked on him. Why hadn't the police arrested them too? He vowed to get even as soon as he saw them again. The reactions were all very similar — threats, revenge, injustice, contempt, surprise, and strong protests of innocence. As I wandered round the jail with my hands behind my back, I began to realise that some of the tabloids had been right. Certain Brits really were a problem for the Spanish — our lager louts were a menace. Nearly all were drunk, all were in trouble and none showed the slightest remorse.

After speaking to a dozen of them I came to one cell, occupied by a different kind of punter. He was about 35, looked like a body-builder and was probably twice the size of the rest. He was wearing just shorts and a vest and his muscle-bound arms were tattooed but I couldn't see exactly his size or his age as he was sitting on the floor of his cell with his face in his hands, blubbering like a baby. A thick moustache peeped through his fingers. 'What's the matter?' I asked, continuing my Prince Charles-type interviews. He kept his face hidden and did not bother answering. 'So what's up?' I asked him again.

'Nothing,' he mumbled. He looked a ridiculous sight. All those around him were rebellious teenagers and here was a weeping grown-up man. He lowered his hands and revealed his red puffy eyes. His white shorts were covered in filth. 'What's up then?' I said. 'What's with the tears? It's really not such a big deal. You'll be out tomorrow anyway, so it can't be that bad.'

'It can,' he said, still blubbering. He had a strong Geordie accent. 'I'm a prison officer at home.'

CHAPTER TEN

Peace and Silence

'You paint a tempting and fascinating picture of San Antonio, Matthew,' said Paul Heiney, once I had finished my report, 'but here's your next assignment... After all those bars and late nights we think you deserve some tranquillity. You're going to have time for reflection this week, because we've arranged for you to join a monastic community at Taizé, near Lyon, in central France... and you're going to be spending a few days there. There will be a challenge though... you're not going to be allowed to talk. You'll be staying in the monastic House of Silence where not a single word is ever spoken. What do you think of that?... Remember no words... Come back and tell us about it next week.'

The biggest inconvenience about living in the monastic House of Silence was not being able to speak when you ate. There were 40 of us in it when I was there and at meals a lot of sign language was used. If you needed the salt, pepper or sugar you pointed and waited for it to be passed to you. Sometimes it seemed to take hours, but you could not just shout at a Brother or a visitor and tell him to 'hurry up and chuck it'. Although no words were ever uttered in the House, meal times could still be very noisy. One day, when we had natural yoghurt for pudding, all you could hear for five or six minutes, was the sound of sugar lumps being crunched (unfortunately they didn't run to granulated) and if someone had indigestion while eating, their sounds reverberated loudly. Luckily, all belching and embarrassing tummy rumbles were politely ignored. Managing to keep my stomach under control, I found the meals very relaxing and, as one who frequently bolts his food while talking at a thousand words a second, also enjoyably beneficial. The good thing anyway was that I did not have to remain silent all the time and could escape the House to talk to other visitors.

Taizé is a famous ecumenical Christian community, 10 kilometres north of Cluny in Burgundy. It was founded in 1940 and its monks are drawn from the Roman Catholic church as well as Protestant denominations. Every summer it attracts thousands of young people who come to live in the community and take part in religious discussion groups. The atmosphere at this time, is rather like that of a big international holiday camp with visitors coming from all over Europe. They stay in tents or dormitories (for those seeking deeper contemplation the *Maison de Silence* is also an option). Some come with their schools, others with church groups, and some just turn up on their own. For Christians seeking spiritual uplift in a sociable, international, religious environment it makes a very interesting break.

Being something of a heathen, I was not sure how I would take to it and having spent the previous week in Ibiza with boozing, bonking Brits, the trip was certainly something different. I must admit, however, it turned out to be a most uplifting experience.

I cannot say that the trip truly put me on the path to righteousness, but each morning I awoke thinking I was in heaven. Every day at 7 a.m. a chorus of angels came and sang to me. That might sound dramatic but that was what the sounds filling the House of Silence sounded like the first time I heard them. Once I had woken up a little, I thought that it was probably the soprano boys' choir getting off to some early-morning practise. It wasn't until the third day that I realised a monk just put on a record and the chorus that filtered through the *Maison de Silence* actually came from a stereo in the kitchen. It remained, however, a lovely, gentle way to start the day.

After getting up and leaving my monastic cell to wash (I was lucky enough to have my own room), it was time for church. The 8 a.m. service was part of the regular routine. We went to church three times every day — morning, afternoon and evening — and if that sounds like overkill it wasn't. The church was a harmonious sanctuary even when empty but, during the services and filled with a thousand people singing beautiful, ancient Latin chants, it had such a calming, uplifting effect that sometimes I did not want to leave.

When not in church, we spent time either in philosophical or religious discussion, or carrying out some of the community's many tasks. These could range from cleaning out the dormitories to peeling several thousand spuds for lunch. The advantage of being in the *Maison de Silence* was that I was not allotted to any particular timetable, which meant I was free to wander round and did not have to participate in too many heavy discussions. I chatted to dozens of different people and was surprised at the great range of visitors. Instead of just a bunch of 'pious goody-goodies' which a prejudiced person might have expected, there were all types of people at Taizé — punks, trendies, studious, rebellious, rich, poor — as well as a dozen nationalities.

I met a boy who felt he had been called to the priesthood and said he needed time for reflection and another who admitted to stealing cars and said he had only come for the girls. I enjoyed my stay there — it certainly made a change from the Costas in Spain —

and if you are interested in visiting Taizé you could combine it with a secular trip around the vineyards. There are some very famous names nearby – Beaune, Mâcon and Gevrey-Chambertin to name just a few.

A couple of years later I was sent on a religious trip again – this time to Mount Áthos, a glorious peninsula jutting out of the north-east corner of the Greek mainland. It is definitely one of the most unique and beautiful places I've ever been to – a theocratic republic, situated on a mountain and self-governed by monks, but, at the same time, remaining part of Greece. It is dotted with monasteries up to a thousand-years-old, bureaucratically complicated to visit (and completely impossible for women). Females have been banned for over a thousand years and the laws restricting them are so strictly enforced that even hens and cows are banned too. Mount Áthos is a farming community but milk and eggs are imported. It is however, a popular destination for Greek men. Many come here on spiritual retreats, some to escape modern life, others maybe just to escape women. In summer only 10 visitors are admitted each day and every one needs a special permit.

After obtaining from the British Consulate in Athens a paper that said I was a genuine reporter, I went to the Greek Foreign Affairs office to collect my visa for Mount Áthos. (If you are foreign and not a journalist, you have to obtain Consulate verification that you have an interest in the Greek Orthodox church, and all visitors must be over 21.) After travelling to Thessaloniki, I took a bus to Ouranopoli, the last town before the holy mountain. I spent the night there and took a boat to Mount Áthos next morning.

When we landed at Dhafni, after two hours at sea, there was yet another bureaucratic hurdle. Our passports were collected and we were told to go to Kariés, a village on Mount Áthos, where we would collect another permit and receive our passports back. Luckily a bus was at the port to take us and when we arrived we were all shown to a small yellow building where we were sold a final permit for 1,000 drachmas. This was the *dhiamonitirion*, the essential piece of paper for visitors to Áthos. With it you are admitted to any of the monasteries free of charge.

I stayed in four different monasteries. The first was Stavronikita, a 90 minute walk from Kariés. I was welcomed by the guest-master who showed me to the dormitory and at 6 o'clock the guests were given supper – bread, smelly cheese and vinegary wine. Afterwards we all went to bed. Everything in Áthos is organised around the sun. Monastery gates are shut at sundown, so you have to make sure you arrive early. At sunrise you get up (which in summer means 4.30 a.m.) and before breakfast you all attend mass. Some services could take over two hours (in beautiful icon-filled and candle-lit chapels), which meant by the time you reached breakfast you were starving. To my surprise wine was also served first thing in the morning (along with tomatoes and bread) and once, on a saint's feast day, our usually frugal meal even included olive oil as well.

There are 1,700 monks on Mount Áthos today. Several hundred years ago there were 20,000. They all come from the Orthodox Church and I met Bulgarians, Russians and Romanians, as well as the majority Greeks. One small monastery I stayed at, Ayios Pantelimon and recognisable by its onion-shaped domes, was known as *lo Roussiko* (the Russian) and inhabited by two dozen Russian monks. The morning mass here was exquisite – chanted in Russian, in a chapel decorated throughout in gold.

Although generally friendly some monks, not surprisingly, disliked visitors. They were bad-tempered when you talked to them and delighted in driving past you on their tractors. I learnt that the correct way to address a monk was with your hands behind your back and that photographing them was not allowed (some, however, were not beyond accepting fees for the privilege). None of them shaved, which meant that some of the older ones had flowing white beards and looked like Merlin the magician. One day I met a Greek man whose son was a monk here – he had not seen his mother for 10 years.

Before leaving I bought a beautiful reproduction icon in Kariés. I got on the boat for Ouranopoli and met two disco owners from Benitses in Corfu. They had both had a hard summer and now with their batteries fully recharged, were ready to join modern Greece again. I would love to return to this medieval world some day.

* If you're a woman and would like to see Mount Áthos, all is not completely lost, as you can see the monasteries on boat-tours from nearby towns, for example Ouranopoli and Ierissos.

CHAPTER ELEVEN

Spanish Encounter

Only a few weeks after meeting the prison officer in Ibiza, I went to Spain yet again – this time for 'The Travel Show Guides'. This was a winter series, made up of programmes dedicated to particular areas, instead of covering a variety of holiday topics. My trip was to Malaga for 'The Guide to the Costa del Sol'. I had finished my work and taken all my pictures when I phoned the office in Manchester to confirm details of my flight back to England. The researcher had bad news. 'I'm afraid we couldn't get you anything from Malaga,' she said. 'You'll have to fly back from Alicante. I'm sorry. That's the best we can do.'

'But that's miles away,' I said. 'How am I expected to get there?'

'You'll have to take a coach. I think there's a couple every day.'

'How long does the journey take?'

'About nine hours but you'll have to buy the ticket and find out the details yourself.' 'Thanks a lot,' I said, and went to the local bus garage. The man at the information desk told me they had a bus leaving that evening which arrived in Alicante the next morning. I phoned the researcher who told me to take it and added that the ticket for my flight, which left the following evening at 9 o'clock, could be picked up before departure from the airport.

I was annoyed that I was having to go to Alicante for two reasons. First, I obviously didn't fancy the coach journey, and second, I was also short of money. After paying for the ticket I only had four-pounds' worth of pesetas left; I was going to have to spend another 30 hours in Spain, and wasn't sure I could make my money last.

At 7 p.m. I got on the bus at Marbella. It had started in

Algeciras, the southern Spanish port from which boats leave for Tangier in Morocco, and was due to make stops at all the towns along the Costa del Sol, before heading directly for Alicante. I chose a seat (there were only a few Moroccans and a couple of Frenchmen on board, so there was plenty of free space) and settled down to try to relax. Various other passengers, mainly Spanish, boarded at the following stops but at Torremolinos a group of German lads, a couple of French girls and a young British bloke got on. The Brit sat down next to me. 'Are you English?' he said. 'Thank God for that. You don't mind if I smoke here, do you?'

I told him I didn't mind and he lit a cigarette — first one, then a second, then another. He seemed very nervous and unable to stop talking. 'So what have you been up to? On holiday? What do you think of Spain? You like it?'

I told him I was tired and wanted to sleep. He said he understood but five minutes later started asking quesions again. 'How long will it take then, this trip? I was told about eight hours…'

He asked me why I was going to Alicante, so I said I was flying back to Gatwick. 'That's exactly what I'm doing,' he replied. 'Although I'm flying into Birmingham. What day are you going back?' I told him the following evening. He said he was leaving two days later.

For the next two hours he would not shut up. He told me he had given up his job and decided to go travelling. He had been in Morocco and was now going to meet friends in Alicante. I told him I was a photographer and that I had been taking pictures for a brochure. 'What a brilliant job,' he said. 'You must get around a bit.' I told him I did a lot of travelling. 'Here,' he said. 'Do you speak any Spanish?'

When I said yes, he asked me if I could help him find a room. 'Nothing too flash, but not too rough either. What's Alicante like for hotels?' I was just about to say that I would not have time when I decided to make a small proposal — I could help him find a room if he bought me breakfast and let me store my bags for the day. 'No sweat,' he said. I told him I was running short of money. He told me not to worry as he still had plenty of cash.

I finally settled down to sleep and the bus arrived in Alicante at seven the next morning. We hauled our bags out of the hold and set off to find a hotel. As we were leaving the bus garage, he rushed into the toilets and came out smoking what, at first, looked like a large cigarette. 'Do you like this stuff then?' He smiled and took it out of his mouth to show me.

Fear and panic ran through my mind. 'Oh God!' I thought. I could see the tabloid headlines in Britain: 'TV Holiday Man in Spanish Drugs Bust.' 'Travel Show Matthew Gets High.'

'No, I don't,' I said nervously. 'It really doesn't interest me at all.'

'Pity,' he said, before adding cryptically, 'cause there's a lot more where that little one came from.'

We found a small hotel without trouble. I now seriously doubted the wisdom in staying with this guy but was so hungry I couldn't stop thinking of the breakfast he would buy me. 'Three thousand pesetas a night for a room here,' I said.

'Great,' he replied. 'Book me in for two nights.' He signed in and I told the owner that I was flying home that night but, for the moment, wanted to leave my bags in this guy's room. 'No problem,' he said and both of us went upstairs.

'Right,' said the young guy. 'I'm just going to have a quick shower and then we'll go and grab a bit of breakfast. I can't wait, I'm starving. God, I stink! I've been wearing these same clothes for a week.' He went into the bathroom and emerged only a few seconds later. He still had his trousers on but his shirt was completely un-buttoned. 'Remember I said it was a pity you didn't smoke that stuff?' he asked.

'Yes,' I said.

'Well, take a look at that,' and he pulled open his shirt to reveal dozens of small greeny-brown packages wrapped around his body with tape. There must have been at least 30 of them. They covered all the flesh from his stomach to his chest and he looked like a wired-up human bomb. 'Not bad is it?' he said proudly. He looked like he might explode at any moment. 'Fifteen or twenty grand's worth, I reckon.'

I was now terrified. 'My job, my passport, the BBC – everything will be finished and I could even go down as an accomplice. I've got to get out of here now,' I thought. The guy could see I was panicking.

'What's up, mate?' he said. 'You must have seen a bit of dope before, haven't you?' The look of horror wouldn't budge from my face. 'Come on, man – it's cool. What would you do if you were unemployed and someone offered you a free holiday? A little trip to Morocco, a boat to Spain and 500 quid in your pocket. What would you do then? All expenses paid? Come on, let's go and have some breakfast. I'll just finish having my wash.' He went back into the bathroom.

I picked up my bags and I flew – out of the room, down the stairs and out of the hotel to the street. I ran through Alicante, careered round the backstreets and didn't even pause to take a breath until I was completely lost in the alleyways. I went into a small bar and bought a glass of mineral water. That left me with the equivalent of less than £2. It was not yet eight-thirty in the morning and my flight home was over 12 hours later. But it was not so much money that I worried about – more, where I could spend the day in Alicante without the guy and his 'friends' bumping into me.

I opened my rucksack. To my delight it was still there – Phil Vallack's naturist *Free Sun Guide to Europe* was sitting on a pair of DM boots.

No one will believe this but I really don't usually take guides to nudist beaches in Europe on my trips, but on this occasion the producer had asked me to check out two naturist beaches near Marbella, so I had chucked it in at the last minute. I looked up mainland Spain... Alicante... page 216... It even had a map to show the area: '*Between Cala de los Judios and Cala de los Cantalares at end of lane from Avenida de la Costa Blanca on the peninsula called Albufereta. Flat slabs of rock with channels of shallow water between.*'

'Perfect,' I thought, 'I can hide between the rocks. They'll never find me on Alicante's nudist beach.'

Unfortunately, from the moment I arrived it started to rain. Luckily, as I had discovered on an earlier trip, a little shower does nothing to deter nudists and a German family arrived only a few minutes later. We got talking when the father asked me why I was searching frantically through my luggage and sniffing all my underpants and socks. I told them about my encounter with the young English guy and said I was terrified that he might have planted something in my bags. After an hour of searching and sniffing, I was finally satisfied that all my possessions were 'clean'.

The Germans offered me some of their picnic which I gratefully accepted and then we went for a swim. At 4 o'clock they gave me a lift into town (I had known these nudists would be friendly) and I took the bus to the airport. I checked in for my flight to Gatwick and arrived in England just after midnight. I've no idea what happened to the guy.

CHAPTER TWELVE

Other Travel Problems

There was more drama on a later trip I made. 'The Travel Show' sent me to New York with instructions to take a Greyhound bus up to Maine to explore the state's pretty fishing villages. That sounded fun but the producer didn't tell me until after we came off air, that for over four months American Greyhound drivers had been engaged in a bitter industrial dispute. Many of them had been sacked after striking, welfare payments were almost non-existent, so feelings were running extremely high. Inexperienced replacements had been given the old drivers' jobs and, according to reports, there had been violent scenes at some Greyhound stations as pickets tried to stop buses travelling.

After a four-hour plane delay I arrived in New York at nine in the evening. I took an airport bus into Manhattan, got off at Port Authority on 41st Street – a notoriously insalubrious place buzzing with much of New York's low-life – and was told that there wasn't a bus north up to Boston until midnight. That bus then arrived two hours late and finally I climbed aboard, passing an uneventful journey through the night, trying to sleep off my jet lag.

The following morning I was woken up at Boston's Greyhound station by the windscreen being pelted with eggs. Pickets screamed and hissed, the driver was booed and jeered and disembarking passengers were surrounded with strikers trying to persuade them not to travel any more with Greyhound. To a chorus of disapproval, I told them I was travelling on a very small budget and unfortunately had no choice.

After breakfast in a nearby diner I boarded another bus north. The scene with the pickets was repeated at other bus garages and, when I arrived in Bangor in the afternoon, I was told that the coastal bus that I had wanted to take to visit the fishing villages, was no longer running because of the strike. There was no choice but to hire a car.

An hour later I was pulling out of Bangor airport in a brand new orange Yugo. It was the cheapest car the local company could offer. I drove up the coast, over a bridge and ended up at Bar Harbor, a tourist town on Mount Desert Island. I had read that the Rockefeller family were among the early vacationers here but today, with its beautiful countryside (most of the island is a National Park), abundant wildlife (it's famous for its chipmunks, racoons and whales) Mount Desert Island (or MDI as it's known locally) is a magnet for thousands of tourists every year seeking a healthy outdoor holiday.

I loved it. I met lots of friendly Americans; went walking, jogging and swimming; hired a mountain bike, went on cycling trails; and had delicious cheap lobsters for breakfast, lunch and dinner. I spent two nights in the cheap local youth hostel (where I met two 18-year-old girls, touring Maine in two new Toyotas that their Dads had bought them for managing to graduate from high school) but the following day, as this was only a four-day transatlantic trip and so much of it was taken up with travelling, I already had to think about starting my tedious journey home.

One thing I had really wanted to do on Mount Desert Island was a whale-watching tour in a boat – these were popular as whales were frequently spotted – but as there wasn't a free tour available until the following afternoon (all the earlier tickets were booked) I settled for a local 'sunset cruise'. This promised to be 'a gentle 90-minute introduction to the beauty of MDI with the possibility of seeing passing seals, ospreys, cormorants and, if you're lucky, pilot whales.' Unfortunately, we had only been at sea for half an hour when we received a distress call on the radio. A local fisherman was in trouble and our skipper decided to go out to sea to try and help him.

Three hours later, in a bouncy force five, I was on my twenty-fourth sick bag (I had eaten two big lobsters for lunch). Passengers were sprawled over the small boat's cabin floor, others were lying on tables and chairs and I was crouched double in my seat. The toilet was permanently engaged. Two men, however – they must have been about 35 – sat through the ordeal smiling and chatting. They knocked back endless cans of Bud beer and chain-smoked their way through packs of Marlboro. The scene would have been comical were it not for the skipper suddenly announcing that the fisherman was still missing, presumed drowned, so we were returning to the harbour. He apologised for everything, told us he would have us back on land in an hour, and promised everyone a free ticket for another 'sunset cruise' the next day. Most of us thought that was very decent of him but when we got back to the harbour, two couples did not think it enough. They demanded a full refund and said they would think about claiming compensation for all the distress they had suffered. I left them protesting on the quay, jumped into my Yugo, and drove my hire car back to Bangor airport.

From there, I took a taxi back to the bus garage and waited for the Boston-bound bus. An hour later there was more drama when our driver, an inexperienced new replacement, crashed it into a building whilst trying to reverse into a small bus garage (and there had not even been any pickets at this one). All the passengers got out, a cop came along to make notes, and the driver went off to ring Greyhound to tell them to send a new bus. 'Bad news folks, I'm afraid,' he said bravely, when he emerged a few minutes later. 'It's gonna be at least two hours before the replacement bus arrives.' It was in fact three hours. That bus arrived along with yet another replacement driver – he was Chinese and had only been doing the job for two days – and just outside Boston he got badly lost when he couldn't work out a one-way system. The advice that passengers kept giving him (in screams from the back of the bus) was fairly useless as he hardly seemed to speak English and we finally arrived in Boston five hours late. I knew then, that if I didn't take the plane to New York, I would miss my flight back to London.

It was rush hour in Boston and it took me an hour to reach Logan Airport in a taxi. I had a wide choice of airlines for New York, but when I went to buy a ticket was told that I hardly had a chance of getting a seat on any of them. The terminal was swarming with navy-blue suited New York businessmen all absolutely desperate to get home. I was sold a stand-by ticket, missed the first couple of flights, and arrived in New York half an hour before my London plane was due to take off. Luckily that was also delayed, so I made it back to Gatwick the following morning, took the train up to Manchester to do the programme, was given my next assignment, and was in Morocco on a school geography field trip high up in the Atlas Mountains, in time for a delicious Arab *tajine* lunch the next day.

CHAPTER THIRTEEN

A Foreign Tourist in Britain

'The Travel Show' decided one week, that having been a tourist in so many different countries, I should experience, firsthand, what it was like to be a foreign tourist in Britain.

'Read out this message please Matthew,' said Penny Junor, 'so that we all think you're a foreigner,' and she handed me a piece of cardboard with a few words written on it. 'Try to say it with a strong German accent.'

'Could you tell me vere ze Tower of London is please,' I said, as Germanically as I could.

'Now in Italian,' said Penny.

'Could-er you-er please-er tell-er me where-er the Tower of London-er is-er please.'

'And now in French,' she said.

'Could you tell me where is zer Tow-er of Lon-don pleeeze.'

'Well, you might get away with it,' said Penny. 'Anyway to give you a bit of help, we're going to give you a disguise and you're to spend the week pretending that you're a foreign visitor to two major British tourist destinations. We're not telling people where you're going, so no one will have any warning, but we want you to see how you are treated and whether, as a tourist, anybody tries to rip you off. Come back next week and tell us how you got on.'

The places they had decided I should visit were London and Brighton. This was great for me as it meant I could spent most of the week sleeping in my own bed. To make sure my disguise was perfect a friend came round to give it a final check. The outfit consisted of glasses, a huge moustache and the make-up department had even gone to the trouble of supplying some false goofy teeth. They made me look hideously ugly and when I first put them in I felt I would choke. 'But the really great thing is that they actually change the shape of your face,' said the head make-up lady.

'It doesn't matter,' said my pal. 'Your most obvious feature is your hairline and you haven't changed that at all.' He ran off to our local market and bought me a fluorescent 'London' tourist baseball hat. 'That's better,' he said. 'You might look a prat but at least no one will have a clue who you are.'

I certainly looked a prat − even more ridiculous than I had on my timeshare adventure − but the great thing about changing your appearance is that you can also change your personality. I was no longer Matthew Collins, so my 'prattishness' didn't matter. I was off to Brighton, but my first stop of the day was my local Blackhorse Road tube station newsagents. When I'm at home I pop into this place every day. It's run in shifts by a variety of couples and on this particular morning John and Joan were behind the counter. I've known these two for about five years and whenever I buy a paper we always have a chat, but this time they treated me like a stranger. I wanted an excuse for buying the *Evening Standard* when I was being a foreigner who hardly spoke English. 'Theatre? Theatre in here?' I asked.

'Oh, yes,' said Joan. 'You'll find everything you want in there. West End, musicals, Shakespeare, drama. It's very good the *Standard* for entertainment.'

'Of course you could take *Time Out*,' added John, suggesting a more expensive option.

'No, this good,' I said. 'This very good. How much?'

'Twen-ty five... pence,' said Joan, pronouncing the words very deliberately.

'Oh... kay...,' I said, sounding like someone with an IQ of six, and I fished in my pocket and pulled out a handful of change − about £15 to be precise. I dangled the coins enticingly under Joan's nose. 'This will be my first test,' I thought.

'Twenty-five pee then, love,' said Joan. I looked at the money pretending that I couldn't understand it. 'Oh... having trouble with our money dear?' said Joan, and very precisely she took out exactly the right change. 'I know − complicated isn't it? Mind you − it used to be worse. There you go love – 25 pence,' and she held out the right coins for me to see.

'Thank you,' I said. 'Well done, Joan,' I thought. 'You've passed the first test with flying colours.'

'You're welcome, darling,' she added, scoring even more points, 'Enjoy your holiday in London.'

I then travelled down to Brighton and when I arrived at the station, immediately jumped in a taxi. 'Hello – could you take me to the pier, please.'

'The pier? Sure, guv,' said the driver and, as far as I could see, he took me by the most direct route and charged me the exact fare on the meter. He dropped me off in front of a man drawing quick caricatures of tourists. I decided to have one done – the artist had enough raw material in me to produce his most outrageous work ever.

'So where are you from then?' he said.

'Oh hell, think of something quickly,' I thought.

'Germany?'

'No, I can't be German – in case he speaks the language himself.'

'Er, Iceland,' I said. ('He'll never speak that,' I thought.)

'Iceland, eh?' he seemed pretty impressed. 'Whereabouts in Iceland? Reykjavik?'

'Yes, Reykjavik,' I said.

'And what's it like there, then? Cold, I suppose?'

'Oh yes, very cold,' I said. After a couple of minutes a crowd had gathered round his easel. Dozens of faces were smiling and chuckling as they examined the cartoon and then cross-referenced it with me. I was longing to see what he had done.

'I bet it's awful,' I thought. 'He's probably getting completely carried away. God knows what he'll make of these teeth.' Five minutes later it was all over. The crowd drifted away and the artist tore off the paper and handed the drawing to me. The caricature was so mild, it was flattering. I was disappointed. Even he had been nice. I paid him his £5 and left.

After the cartoon, I decided it was time to test the friendliness of the locals. I asked dozens of different people directions. 'Excuse me,' I said to a group of young lads. 'Could you please tell me way to the station.'

'Sure, mate,' said one, and he gave me clear, explicit directions and even repeated them, putting his hand on my shoulder, pointing the right way with the other and talking extremely slowly, to make sure I had really understood him. I asked other people – teenage girls, teenage boys, housewives and a policeman. All demonstrated the same high level of friendliness and courtesy and it made me feel pleased that tourists here were treated very well. But then I met some old ladies having a gossip near the pier.

'Excuse me,' I said interrupting them. 'How to go to the station please?'

'Have you got a map then?' asked one tersely.

'Map?' I said, looking confused.

'Yes, map,' said another. 'So we can show you where you're going.'

'No, sorry,' I said, 'No map.'

'Well, stupid him,' muttered another under her breath. 'You'd think he'd at least have a map.'

'All right,' said the leader. 'Well, you see where that clock tower is over there...' and she proceeded to give me the most complicated, imprecise directions anyone had given me all day. When she was finished I stood with my mouth open-wide.

'Just look at him,' muttered another old dear. 'What an expression. He hasn't got a clue what you said, Jean. And he hasn't got a clue where he's going.'

'Understand?' said the leader.

'Er... maybe,' I said. 'Possibly... er... please... repeat please.'

She machine-gunned her instructions out again before one of the others said, 'Jean dear, I just wouldn't bother.'

I left them tutting about me by the pier and went for some food in a nearby pizzeria. Perhaps it was my appearance or maybe my stupid foreign manner, but the waitress there seemed to take an instant dislike to me. I ordered a beer and a 'Quattro Stagioni' with extra peppers and cheese. She brought it very quickly and I ordered a salad. She served that, so I ordered some garlic bread. She brought that, so I ordered another beer. She served that, so I ordered my pudding. She had been so unfriendly I rather unkindly decided that I would keep her on her toes and test her patience. She thought I hardly spoke English. 'Can we have some ice-cream for that horrible creep over there,' she bawled as she entered the kitchen. 'He's driving me absolutely mad.' Of course I understood every word.

Apart from the old ladies and the pizzeria waitress, the locals of Brighton were most friendly. I bought ice-creams and candy floss, took several different taxis and not one person tried to rip me off. Next stop was London. 'I'm bound to get fleeced there,' I thought.

Through the BBC press office a meeting with a reporter from *The Sun* had been arranged. Apparently he wanted to do a story about my assignment and our PR man thought it would be good publicity for the programme. We met at the Houses of Parliament after I had already spent the morning posing as a tourist from Iceland. 'So what's the score, then?' said the reporter. 'London tourist rip-offs job, is it?'

'Well, actually,' I said. 'Everyone's been very honest. I haven't been ripped off at all yet.'

'You're joking,' he replied with surprise. 'No £5 ice-creams? No £20 taxi rides?'

'Not at all. I've taken half a dozen taxis and all the drivers were honest. I've bought four ice-creams — no one has overcharged me — and I've constantly held out great piles of change and everyone has taken the correct amount.'

'Blimey,' he said. 'So it's a "London's the Tops for Tourists" story, then?'

'Well, maybe,' I said. 'So far, it's been like that anyway.'

'Right then,' he said, 'Let's see you in action.'

I spent the next couple of hours with him, buying ice-creams, souvenirs and postcards; taking taxis and asking Londoners directions. The treatment was always the same — friendly, honest and fair. 'Well it really is a "London's the Tops" story then,' said the reporter. When we had finished, he went back to *The Sun's* HQ in Wapping but when I phoned him a few hours later, to find out when it was going in the paper, he told me the story had been 'spiked'. 'Sorry — too nice really,' he said. 'Just wasn't spicy enough.'

I had another day in London in my 'Torvil from Reykjavik' outfit but the results were always the same — honest taxi drivers, generally helpful locals, and straight-laced Italian ice-cream sellers. Reactions were almost boring and predictable. When I asked for receipts some drivers offered to double them and when I refused one chap even said: 'You're an honest gentleman, you are sir – not like some of the other foreign visitors I get in here. They ask me to put down some very inflated sums. Where exactly are you from sir? Iceland? You must be honest people, you Icelandics.' And when I took a taxi from half-way down the Strand to Trafalgar Square, a two-minute ride, the driver muttered under his breath, 'lazy git' but still didn't over-charge me.

Although the treatment I received seemed almost too good to be true (this was 1991, the summer after the Gulf War, and numbers of foreign visitors to London were down so that probably had a big influence) I did meet a few real tourists who complained about being ripped-off. One poor American, in his twenties, had been taken from Piccadilly Circus to a Soho peep-show (via Kings Cross) then made to pay £100 for a whisky ('I had no choice,' he said, 'these big guys weren't going to let me out'). Other Americans complained about being fleeced by ticket-touts outside the big musicals, and several different tourists told me how unlicensed mini-cab drivers, who had approached them at Victoria station, had offered cheap rides, put their cases in the car boot, then threatened to make off with their luggage if they did not pay an extortionate fare. In general though, the portrait was good. I certainly had nothing but praise for the many taxi drivers I used and said so on the programme the next week. 'London taxi drivers were marvellous,' I told Penny. That made it all the more ironic when only a couple of days later, a driver tried to charge me £25 for taking me from Heathrow to Hillingdon. 'But it's only down the road,' I protested. He said it was out of his zone. I refused to pay. We came to a disagreeable compromise and once he'd snatched my money, he said 'scum like me' were people London taxi drivers 'could well do without'.

CHAPTER FOURTEEN

The Survival Course

Whenever they requested 'ideas for Matthew' on the programme they always received suggestions that worried me. Many were unsuitable and others just downright sadistic. One area I always treated with caution was anything to do with the military. A particularly unpleasant trip was organised along army lines – a survival weekend on the Scottish Isle of Lewis that I would not recommend to anyone.

I met my instructor one Saturday morning in a pub in the island's capital, Stornoway. He told me he was an ex-army corporal and that he had been a sniper for nearly 11 years. That sent a few shivers down my spine; then he said said that although I would theoretically be spending the weekend alone, he would always have me in his sights. I'm sure it was a slip of the tongue, but for hours after he had left me, I could feel cross hairs burning into my back.

He gave some background about the course. 'For the purposes of this exercise, we're going to pretend that you're a lost mountaineer and that you find yourself in different environments – one inland and one by the sea-shore. Of course, if you like, we could imagine you've just survived an air crash, but in both scenarios your attitude and survival skills will be what ensure you don't die. I'm going to give you some equipment, but basically you'll be living off whatever the local terrain can offer. Have a big lunch. It'll be your last proper meal for 48 hours so I would enjoy it if I were you.'

Feeling like a condemned man, I chose fillet steak. Then he went through the equipment he was giving me – a first-aid kit, flints, cotton wool, waterproofs, some fishing line with hooks, a bivvy bag, a water filter and a piece of plastic sheeting.

We finished lunch and, laden with our packs, walked out of

Stornoway into the countryside. The course started immediately. 'Pay attention to all the local flora and fauna,' he said, 'and put some nettles and coltsfoot in a bag. They will make a nice stew for dinner.' For the next three hours we walked without stopping and I learnt about some other survival dishes. 'Ever eaten worms?' he asked. 'Cause you will this weekend. Don't worry, they're quite nice − better than slugs. Why not put a few in your bag?'

One problem on the Isle of Lewis, I learnt, is that there is very little vegetation suitable for making a fire. 'So we're going to have to swim through a channel to another small island where we'll find plenty of trees.' The sun was sinking fast and the wind was beginning to blow. 'Take off your clothes and pack everything into the plastic bivvy bag. Try not to get anything wet.' I tied them all up in a bundle and arrived on the island naked and shivering. 'So here we are,' he said. 'I'll show you how to make a fire and collect some water then I'll leave you on your own.'

It took me an hour to get a fire going and, after struggling desperately with my flints, I was furious to see him light a cigarette with his lighter. 'Done it all before,' he said. 'So I've got to have a few perks, haven't I?' Collecting water was easy, as there were puddles everywhere (it rains all the time on Lewis as I was about to find out) but even after putting it through my simple water filter it still tasted absolutely foul. 'Sheep droppings,' said the instructor. 'The water's always full of them here. I should boil it as well.' We shared a delightful supper of coltsfoot and nettles − really quite tasty − but I declined the offer of worms. I did not feel ready for them yet. 'Don't know what you're missing,' he said.

After supper he left me on my own. It was about 10 o'clock. I took the equipment out of my small bivvy bag and constructed a simple shelter from the square of plastic sheeting. (I had to take the laces out of my boots to tie it to some overhanging branches.) Then I crawled into my bivvy bag and tried to settle down for the night. Unfortunately there was a small pool at the bottom of my bag and even with my boots on, my feet were soon soaking wet. But this was still luxury compared with my state two hours later.

Shortly after I'd tried to shut my eyes, it had begun to rain. Then the wind started howling. My shelter blew off and landed in a puddle and my bivvy bag rapidly filled up with rain. I went to put

▲ *Preserving my modesty at the nudist camp*

Running for the Lloret bus — leg-in-plaster trip ▼

▲ A tuna fish lunch at the end of a nightmare coach ride

Trying to hitch a lift on a yacht – Siracusa, Sicily ▼

▲ *Five star accommodation in Italy*

Enjoying selling ice-creams in St. Tropez ▼

▲ Hitch-hiking with a bicycle in France

Disguised as a foreign tourist in London ▼

▲ *Propping in Ibiza — getting girls into burs*

Surviving on Lewis ▼

▲ *Swedish experience with Charlotte Anderson*

Enjoying life on the raft ▼

▲ *Slide styling treatment — Austrian health farm*

Aboriginal rock paintings ▼

▲ *The end of a day's riding — Sierra Nevada, Spain*

Meeting (a cardboard) Gorbachev in Moscow ▼

on the waterproofs and found to my horror that the leggings had not been included. I was wearing jeans, so my legs soon got soaked and I did not have a spare pair of trousers (you might think jeans were stupid clothes to take on a survival course but, as usual, I had not known what I would be doing that week for 'The Travel Show'). I took off my jeans, put my DM boots back on and ran on the spot for a while (to keep my circulation going) hoping that the rain would soon stop. But the downpour continued all night. To try to stay warm I went for a walk and after pacing increasingly deeper into the undergrowth, I came across a neat little tent. Loud contented snores were coming out of it; I returned to my bivvy bag in furious frustration and tried again to sleep, but it was impossible. The rain was relentless and my clothes, skin and bones were all soaked. Dawn finally broke just as the rain began to stop. I went back to the instructor's tent. He was still snoring and did not emerge until six-thirty.

I was incensed when I peeked in his tent. He had a proper down-filled sleeping-bag, a lamp and a pile of army rations – porridge, soup, teabags and peas. When he got up he put on a full set of waterproofs and wrapped a pair of gaiters round his boots. 'Sleep well?' he said. 'Right then, let's have a bit of breakfast.'

'I'll have some porridge and a tea please,' I replied.

'Well, officially, of course, that's not allowed... but seeing it's you I'll give you some.' He poured out a tea and gave me some porridge in a mess tin. As day two was to be spent in a sea-shore environment we packed up our things after breakfast and headed for a beach on the other side of the island. 'Why do we have to walk,' I asked. 'Can't we just stay stranded here?'

He said that, for the purposes of the course, we had to get to know the different terrains; and when we had reached the small beach he explained the food available there. 'Right,' he said. 'You've got plenty of fish, obviously. Try and use your line and hook. Worms make good bait, so do little sea-snails and, of course, you can eat these too. Full of nourishment. You might be tempted by the birds but I'm afraid these are all out of bounds and even though there are sheep everywhere, these are all privately owned so you have to keep your hands off them too. Good luck. Any questions? I'll see you in 24 hours.'

I placed my damp possessions under some trees behind the beach. I was worried my camera would be ruined. Any instinct I had to survive was fuelled exclusively by anger. 'The producer's not going to hear the last of this,' I kept muttering to myself. 'Of all the ridiculous things to do. And I didn't even have any warning. I only had jeans, shorts and swimming trunks packed and here I am on a remote Scottish island. He's going to have a piece of my mind when I get back. And I expect an easy trip next week. If I get pneumonia I'm definitely going to sue. But I'm going to survive, just to get my own back on him. Swine – he's probably reading the Sunday papers back in his comfortable Cheshire home. I wish there was a phone box near this beach.'

I wandered down to the sea to have a go at fishing but it was hopeless – nothing was interested in my bait. I had a few stinging nettles left and they did for lunch but by 4 o'clock I was starving. I walked along the beach and picked up some sea-snails from the sand. After an hour I managed to light a fire and threw a few sea-snails into the mess tin. They retreated immediately into their shells and looked so pathetic that I took them out quickly and put them back on the beach. Then I thought I'd try the worms that I'd collected with the plants the day before. I took the bag containing them out of my pocket, emptied it and braced myself to pop a little wriggling thing in my mouth. But I couldn't manage that either. I threw them over my shoulder towards some trees.

Night came and of course it started to rain. I was worried my fire would go out. Once I had collected all the driftwood on the beach I started to rip down some trees. I was now even angrier. 'What's that squaddie doing?' I thought. 'Probably reading a dirty book in the comfort of his goose-down sleeping-bag.'

The night passed agonisingly slowly. The rain was relentless again and the fire flickered down to a weak glow. Just as it was about to go out I decided there was only one thing to do. I ripped up my notebook and threw it on to the embers. Then I added a James Herbert novel that the author himself had given me (I had been on a radio show with him the week before), 'Sorry James,' I thought. Next the plastic sheet and some films went on and, as I was still freezing and the remaining embers went almost dead again, I decided I had one final option – I took off my socks (they were soaking wet anyway) and bunged them on the fire. They provided fifteen minutes' warmth. Had it not eventually stopped raining I probably would have added my jeans, shirt and bivvy bag. But luckily the sun raised its lovely head.

I finished the last of the nettles for breakfast and drank some sheep-dung flavoured water. I spent the rest of the morning running round the beach to keep warm, mumbling to myself and working out I would say to the producer. I was going to make sure I gave him hell. At 10 o'clock the instructor bounded over and told me I had passed the survival course with flying colours.

'Don't you feel good then?' he asked. 'That you've really proved something to yourself?'

'Yes,' I said sockless and soaked. 'I must be a cretin to do my job.'

CHAPTER FIFTEEN

A Battlefield Tour

As it was so unpleasant and frustrating, the Scottish Islands survival course remains permanently engraved on my mind, but another military experience was even more memorable because I found it so moving. In fact the trip had such an emotional effect on me that I had to hide my tears when I made my report later on television. It was a battlefield tour to the Somme in northern France and our visit coincided with the 75th anniversary of the start of the First World War's most infamous battle.

A battlefield tour is, literally, a tour to a battlefield. Over the last few years these have become increasingly popular and whereas many of the specialist companies, such as Holts' Tours, started doing trips only to famous World War sites, they now cover battlefields all over the globe, including those of the Napoleonic, Boer, Zulu and American Civil Wars.

The Somme trip, however, remains one of the most popular. This northern French site was the scene of a bloody mass slaughter. When the original British orders to start the battle were given, the intention was to break the stalemate in the war by bombarding the German trenches, capturing their land and quickly advancing. Unfortunately the plans were not fulfilled. The Battle of the Somme started on 1 July 1916 and dragged on until 17 November of that year. During the course of it 400,000 young British men were lost — one for every square yard of territory gained.

People go on battlefield tours for a variety of reasons. Many have relations who were lost in the battle, so for them it is a special personal pilgrimage. Others are interested in the historical aspects and approach the tour from an academic angle. On my bus were all these different kinds of people, as well as a few regular soldiers and a contingent from the Royal Hampshire Regiment's Ex-Servicemen's Association, which included two sprightly men of 95, Ernie and George, who had actually fought in the Battle of the Somme.

We started our tour in a hotel outside Amiens and the day after arriving were woken at 5 a.m. We dressed, boarded our coach and were driven to the site of the battle. During the 45-minute journey, Major and Mrs Holt cleverly created an atmosphere of war, starting with pre-battle optimism. Flickering, jerky images of bright-faced, smiling soldiers proudly going to fight for King and Country were played on the coach's on-board video; cassettes of famous First World War songs came over the sound-system – 'It's a Long Way to Tipperary', 'Pack Up Your Troubles in Your Old Kit Bag', 'Keep the Home Fires Burning' – and some passengers joined in the singing. Then Mrs Holt changed the mood by reading out letters and World War One poems. The most moving lines were by a mother talking to her son about what they would do when he was older. 'Of course her boy did not get older,' said Mrs Holt. 'Like thousands of others he was slaughtered on that day.'

By the time we got off the coach the mood of everyone was sombre. I had a lump in my throat. My imagination and emotions were heightened and the grassy plain before us took on the atmosphere of a battlefield.

It was now seven-fifteen in the morning and our group was going to simulate 'going over the top' just as the Tommies had done, 75 years ago on that day. 'Going over the top' described the nightmarish act of climbing out of the trenches, going into unoccupied 'no man's land', and advancing towards the enemy's territory. The Battle of the Somme started precisely at 7.28 a.m. when 17 mines were blown under the German front line and two minutes later, at 7.30 precisely, the order was given for 60,000 British soldiers, ridiculously over-burdened with packs, rifles, gas masks, spades, water-bottles, empty sandbags and grenades to advance towards enemy positions. We climbed into the remains of the trenches and Mrs Holt gave each of us a small tot of rum, just as the NCOs had done to all the men minutes before they went into battle. I felt a warm sensation in my stomach and thought of those boys, who on a similar, French summer's day, were about to be mown down in hails of gunfire.

At seven-thirty we tourists started our advance and walked out of the trenches across the field. Most people were silent, lost in their thoughts, but others made jokes and laughed a lot. Nobody criticised them however. The mixed moods reflected those expressed at the time, and humour, Major Holt said later on the coach, was always a shield in times of war. When we reached the end of the field, a trek that took us just a few minutes, but which took the British several weeks, we all felt a sense of relief – from the emotions that had gripped us and from the fact that we had been lucky enough not to have been born in time for the battle.

At 8 o'clock we went for breakfast in the Burma Star, a incongruously named French café in Pozières. The café had existed during the First World War and the *patronne* greeted us just as her predecessor must have greeted previous British customers three-quarters of a century earlier. We settled down for *croissants* with *chocolat chaud* or *café au lait* and examined the decorations on the walls – pieces of shrapnel, faded old photographs, medals, certificates and grenades. Afterwards we went for a trip to a First World War cemetery which was a moving and humbling experience. Endless rows of headstones fill immaculate, tranquil gardens and the inscriptions on them are terrifyingly similar: 'Private John Graham – Died 1.7.1916 – Aged 19 Years.' 'Private Wilfred Turner – Died 1.7.1916 – Aged 18 years.' The sacrifice and waste is visible for all to see (and I stood next to an 18-year-old boy who could hardly believe that boys as young as him had been slaughtered in such vast numbers) but I also found myself experiencing a sense of homage to the thousands of men lying there. I thought of my grandfather – a man I never knew – who, at one point survived a battle, along with only 25 others, in which 500 British men were killed.

As a balance to our perceptions of the Great War we also visited a German cemetery as the uncle of one lady in our group had died fighting for the 'enemy' side. She found his grave, laid down some flowers and returned to the coach where she read out a letter to his mother. The German lady translated for us: 'Dear Mum,' it said. 'I hope you and the family are all well. Please could you send me some bacon and socks for Christmas as rations are going down and it is cold.' The letter proved what everybody knew – that the German soldiers' suffering was no different from British Tommies' hardships.

One of the fascinating aspects of a battlefield tour is that many people who go on them are able to trace personal links with the battles and these then provoke further interest. When I returned home I asked my father to give me more details of his father. He produced some papers and, going through them one afternoon, we found our own pieces of family history. There were no letters from my grandfather but a pile of faded papers dated from 1917-19 were addressed to '*Mon cher Tommy*' (his name was Thomas) – he had had a French war-time girl-friend.

After the cemeteries we went to the official 75th Anniversary Remembrance Ceremony at Thiepval and then to a reception at Bray-sur-Somme where we had lunch in the civic hall. As well as local dignitaries there were French and British survivors from the battle. I sat next to George and asked him what it was like at the time. 'Well,' he said, 'It wasn't very pleasant. You lost a lot of friends and felt the bullets go whistling past you.' But he didn't really want to talk about the war. He was a keen amateur photographer and country-and-western music lover and preferred to discuss cameras and Dolly Parton records.

CHAPTER SIXTEEN

Swedish Experience

Having been told by Penny Junor that, for the timeshare assignment I had to find myself a girl-friend, it was pleasantly surprising to learn that, for a later trip, 'The Travel Show' was going to supply one – a Swedish girl-friend at that...

'This week,' said Penny, 'you're flying to Gothenburg. From the airport you drive to Gunnerud in the beautiful region of Värmland. Here you'll be met by Charlotte Anderson . . . who's going to help you build a raft. You'll spend the next week on the raft together, floating down part of the River Klarälven (a 400-kilometre river which flows from Norway to Sweden) passing through mountains and pine forests. You'll see plenty of wildlife – beavers, mink, kingfishers, heron and maybe even some moose. Charlotte will be your guide. Have a great time. Come back and tell us about it next week.'

I love trips on rivers – travelling on water is usually so relaxing – but this one had the exciting prospect of an unknown Swedish female companion. For the next 12 hours I could hardly stop wondering what Charlotte Anderson would be like.

After arriving in Gothenburg I drove around the massive Lake Vänern to the Värmland region and arrived at an outdoor centre in Gunnerud. It was full of blonde, healthy-looking Nordic boys taking canoes and inflatable dinghies out of sheds. A tall blonde girl in a bikini top and cut-off jeans, with a large knife hanging from her belt, was supervising them. She came over and shook my hand. I immediately thought of Ursula Andress in the James Bond film *Doctor No*.

'Matthew Collins? Pleased to meet you. Welcome to Värmland. Come with me please.' Charlotte was business-like and asked if I had ever built a raft. When I said no she gave me a lecture on skills I needed to construct one. 'You can tie knots?' she asked. I said I couldn't – apart from a reef-knot learnt in Cubs. 'Well, your reef-knot will be useful. But you also need half-hitches and clove-hitches.' She gave me a demonstration. 'Everything clear now?' I said yes even though it wasn't. 'Okay,' she said. 'Get in the van. We'll collect our equipment then drive to Branasang. There we will find logs for the raft.'

When we had loaded the van with wooden boxes containing our week's requirements – a camping stove, pots, pans, plates, cutlery, provisions, a lifebelt, and some tarpaulin – we drove through the village to the river bank where thousands of logs were piled up high. Several other people were already there – a group of German scouts, a Swedish family with two teenage children, and a middle-aged German man with his young wife. 'He is a millionaire,' whispered Charlotte. 'He comes here every year and travels in his own private plane. He spends half his life in luxury hotels but says that floating on the raft is the best way to relax.'

Charlotte greeted them and showed the first-timers how to start. 'Okay – take all the big logs and put them on the bottom. They float best so they provide a buoyant base. Secure them using the knots you have been shown and build up the base from different layers.' After an hour the German businessman had almost finished and was anxious to set sail but I was having problems with my hitches. 'This is a half-hitch and this is a clove-hitch,' said Charlotte. She cut off some rope with her frighteningly sharp knife and gave me a demonstration again.

Soon, with the base and a frame for shelter completed, the German businessman and his wife were ready. They pulled the tarpaulin over the upright logs, loaded their equipment and pushed their raft into the river. '*Auf Wiedersehen,*' they said and began to drift slowly down-river. The scouts went next but after four hours I was still struggling with my knots.

'I show you one final time,' said Charlotte and after helping me with the hitches and the rest of the logs we were finally ready to go. We were to float down a 100-kilometre stretch of the river back to Gunnerud. Charlotte reckoned it flowed at two kilometres an hour so the trip would take four days. We pushed the raft out and began our leisurely sail.

Although the scenery was stunning and the gentle movement of the raft relaxing, all I could think about was how I would get on with my companion. What would we do when it came to pulling over for the night? Would she make me sleep in a separate tent? Or would she fulfill old, silly schoolboy fantasies about Swedish women? I dangled my feet over the edge of the raft and thought about all the possibilities.

It wasn't long before I found out. At 6 o'clock we pulled over to the bank. Shouting instructions to me to watch the stern, Charlotte navigated us in with a small paddle. She unpacked the stove, took out some bread and tins, and started cooking. Then she took out three plates. 'Three?' I quizzed.

'Yes,' she said. 'My boy-friend is eating with us too.' Minutes later he arrived on a bicycle. The rendezvous spot had obviously been well chosen as, even though the river was separated from the road by a forest, Peter found us immediately. Charlotte introduced us. We shook hands and sat down to dinner.

After the meal Peter took out a small tin which contained something looking like snuff. I thought it a strange habit for a young man but instead of putting it up his nose, he rolled some into a ball, placed it under his upper lip and started simultaneously to suck and chew. 'You know this?' he asked. 'We call it *snus* – a mixture of tobacco, glass and special things. Like cigarettes it gives you nicotine but you don't have to breathe it through your lungs. The glass breaks little veins in your mouth and the nicotine enters your bloodstream. It is very pleasurable and relaxing. Try some please...' I took a dab on my finger and placed it in my mouth. 'Suck slowly and the glass will work gently through your mouth.'

Two minutes later I was feeling dizzy. I spat the stuff out when it began to taste foul and thought I would fall off the raft. 'So it can't be legal?' I asked.

'Sure,' replied Peter defiantly. 'That's why many Swedes don't want us in the European Union. They worry that if we join, Brussels will make *snus* illegal and then we will lose an old Swedish custom.'

'Show him the hole in your lip,' said Charlotte. 'He has no flesh where the glass has worked its way through the skin. Soon he will have to use his lower lip.' Peter curled up his top lip to reveal a revolting brown and purple hole. Charlotte explained he had been using *snus* for over 10 years and that this was frequently the result. She had tried it but did not like it much, although many Swedish women still used *snus*. 'You can get it in different flavours. I liked the brandy one,' she said.

For the rest of the evening Peter sat chewing and spitting like Huckleberry Finn, and we talked about Britain and Sweden. I suggested we buy some beer but they said it was far too expensive. At 10 o'clock, just as dusk fell, we prepared for bed. We cleaned our teeth from saucepans, then they got into their double sleeping-bag, while I found a space on the edge of the raft. I then stuffed in my ear-plugs (I always carry some for emergencies — usually for hotel rooms near discos and mosques, not love-rafts on the River Klarälven) and crawled into my single sleeping-bag. Early next morning Peter got up, quietly made breakfast and cycled off to do a day's work.

The following evening he returned and we met him at another, obviously pre-arranged point. After baked beans, bread and cheese Peter rounded the meal off with *snus*. They then settled down into their double sleeping-bag and I, once again, stuffed in my ear-plugs, crawled to the edge and got into my cold, single one.

So the trip may not have been as exciting as I hoped — no Swedish girls, extremely basic food, and hardly a can of lager all week (although I did find a shop that sold the low-alcohol stuff) but it was nevertheless very enjoyable. During the day we watched the scenery change from mountains to pine forest. We also swam, fished (Charlotte caught a grayling which we ate), paddled a canoe (which we had towed) and watched beavers follow the raft — they would bash the water with their tails to tell us we were in their territory. We saw kingfishers, herons and were even visited by a mink — he scurried aboard before spotting us and running off.

Our only problems were rocks or whirlpools. We had to punt or paddle our way out of trouble but this was rare as our map showed most hazards (and when we did get into whirlpools Charlotte soon paddled us out of them). We passed through a few tiny villages but the only other sign of civilisation was the odd shop. Peter visited every evening and always left the following morning (each day he had further to cycle to work) but after four days of relaxing, we unleashed the raft and the logs floated away towards a paper mill.

The moment I got back to England, people kept asking me the same question: 'So how did you get on with Charlotte?'

'Brilliant,' I said. 'She reminded me of Ursula Andress.' I did not mention Peter as well.

CHAPTER SEVENTEEN

Europe in a Week

Having relaxed on some assignments many others nearly burnt me out. One of these was a whirlwind tour with an Inter-rail ticket. These are a brilliant idea – for around £250 they give unlimited travel for a month on most of the railways in Europe. Up until 1991, however, they had only been available for people under the age of 26. I had made several Inter-rail tours as a student in my teens and early twenties. They were all great fun – but as I got older and passed the age limit, I thought such trips were behind me. Then a new ticket for people over 26 was introduced and 'The Travel Show' decided to buy one. But instead of giving me a month to 'do' Europe they decided a week was enough.

'You're going to Paris,' said Penny Junor. 'But your schedule is tight. You travel to Brussels, Amsterdam, Berlin, Prague, Vienna, Venice and then Paris. We want to know about life on the rails – how different European trains compare – and how to have the perfect Inter-railing holiday. Come back next week and tell us all about it.'

I was furious. I was nearing the end of a summer series and had already had three months of constant travel. I certainly did not fancy living in train carriages for a week and besides, felt that Inter-railing round Europe in only a week was not the kind of thing that any sane person would try to do. I left the studio an angry man. I was setting off the following morning for Brussels but first had to travel down to London.

As I had an early departure, the producer had made one concession – he had booked me a room at the Scandic Crown

Hotel, next to Victoria Station. It was so convenient that it was only a two-minute walk from the platforms for International departures. I wasn't looking forward to my trip but the prospect of staying here pleased me because, as I live in London, I had never stayed in one of the capital's hotels. I rang Amanda, an old girl-friend, and invited her to dinner at the Scandic.

She found it strange coming up to my room. 'I feel like a tart,' she said, as I opened the door. 'Come on, let's get some food.' The restaurant was full of Scandinavians and Germans with only the odd British diner. We ordered our meal but half-way through the first course I shut my eyes and winced in panic.

'What's the matter?' Amanda asked.

'I haven't done my VAT return and I'm already a month late. If I don't do it this week they'll probably send round the bailiffs.' I had heard terrible stories about what happens if you don't pay VAT on time. As I work for so many different people (the BBC has only ever employed me on short contracts) I am classed as self-employed and have to charge VAT on all the jobs I do. Every three months I fill in a Return and pay the money that I charged in VAT back to Customs and Excise. It's a bureaucratic hassle and because I travel often it just adds to the piles of paperwork that build up at home.

I bolted the rest of my food, ordered a coffee and hurriedly said goodnight to poor Amanda. Then I ran out of the hotel, jumped on the tube and rushed back to my Walthamstow flat. I was there for the next four hours trying to calculate how much I owed in VAT. At 3 a.m. I had finally finished so I ordered a minicab and returned to the Scandic Crown.

'You live in Walthamstow but you stay in Victoria hotel,' said the driver. He was a young Asian boy, only about 19, and seemed to find it suspicious.

'I'm not even staying the night now,' I said. I didn't want to spoil his excitement. 'I'll only have a couple of hours there.'

I returned to my room and finally went to bed. Ninety minutes later the phone rang. 'Good morning, sir,' said a bright female voice. 'This is your morning alarm call.'

'Thanks,' I said and fell asleep again. But 10 minutes later there was a 'peep, peep, peep' as my own back-up service went off.

The journey to Dover was reasonably comfortable. They are so busy in summer that many trains to the Channel ports have 'reserved' stickers slapped on most carriages but I found a free seat among an Italian school party. It was noisy but at least I could sit. I shut my eyes and dozed off immediately.

There was bad news on arrival – the hydrofoil to Ostend was delayed. Apparently there were storms in the Channel.

Forty minutes after the scheduled departure time we all went aboard. I had never been on a cross-channel hydrofoil before, so this was another new experience.

It is not one I shall repeat however, at least not in bad weather. I often get seasick, although this time I was fine, but we had only been at sea a few minutes when we started bouncing violently up and down. Dozens of passengers began to throw up and the poor Belgian stewardesses distributed sick-bags then collected all the used ones. As if these duties were not enough they also produced ice-packs which they placed on the necks of puking passengers.

'What service,' I thought. 'I'll have to get a shot so I can mention it on the programme.' But when I asked passengers with ice-packs on their necks if I could take their picture for 'The Travel Show' none of them, not surprisingly, obliged.

When we arrived at Ostend I found I had missed my first train but that didn't worry me. Instead I felt pleased. 'What a shame.' I thought. 'If it goes on like this I won't get round Europe in a week.'

Two hours later I was having lunch on the Grand' Place in Brussels. Belgian food was such an enjoyable discovery that I missed my connection to Amsterdam. This was worrying as it was completely my fault. 'Oh well,' I thought, 'I won't bother with Amsterdam. I'll miss it and go straight to Berlin.'

When I arrived, I quickly found a cheap hotel (it was simple – I just went to a local tourist office, they gave me some names and prices, took a deposit, then phoned through an instant reservation) and decided to give a Polish friend a ring.

Maria had only been in Berlin for three weeks. We had met a couple of summers before at Lake Ballaton in Hungary, and later kept in touch through frequent postcards. She was hoping to find work as a make-up artist but at this time was working as a cleaner. We arranged to meet in a café and to my astonishment, after ordering a coffee, she suggested we went to a peep-show.

'Why ever do you want to see one of those, Maria?' I asked, amazed at this suggestion from such a sweet Polish girl.

'Because I have never seen one before. They don't have them in Warsaw. Here, in Berlin, they are everywhere and I'm curious to see what they're like.' I told her I didn't think it a good idea but she kept saying how curious she was.

Soon I succumbed. 'All right,' I said. 'But I have got loads of other things to do. This is a trip for the British Broadcasting Corporation. When Penny Junor asks me what I did in Berlin, I can't say I spent my time in peep-shows.'

We left the café and made for the sleazy streets. Peep-shows were soon everywhere. 'You go in,' I said. 'I'll wait outside. Some English tourists might recognise me and then I'll be in trouble with my producer.'

'Please Massew, you come in too,' she said. And Maria hauled me into a sex shop. She bolted us into a cubicle and excitedly put a mark in the coin slot. A window shutter slid open to reveal a pale, flabby, badly bruised woman, gyrating naked on the floor. Maria watched her, open-mouthed, but a couple of minutes later the window shutter slid closed again. 'Quick, quick,' she said. 'Put in another mark.' I put in two more then said I'd had enough. When we emerged outside she was breathless with excitement. 'How can they do that?' she asked.

The following morning I met Maria again. We walked to the Brandenburg Gate, which two years before had been in East Germany. All around it were Turks and Eastern Europeans selling whatever they could. A Romanian offered us some matches, a Pole some Russian army hats, and a Turk offered us a bit of Berlin Wall – wrapped in plastic with a certificate of authenticity. 'Don't bother,' said a young Australian, 'Everyone knows that comes from Istanbul.'

After lunch in the former East Berlin I had to think about Prague. I took out my timetable and looked up some trains. I had a choice – I could either leave early that afternoon or take a train 12 hours later. I decided to take the late-night service and to spin out more time in Berlin.

We spent the remains of the day sightseeing – Checkpoint

Charlie and the Museum of the Wall. We also saw the Reichstag, the old German parliament building and the Kaiser-Wilhelm Gedächtniskirche — the famous church which, after terrible bombing during the war and the destruction of all the buildings around it, steadfastly refused to collapse — and we visited the Pergamon Museum, a fantastically stocked home to Roman and Ancient Egyptian artefacts which include a perfect bust of Nerfitite. At midnight we went to Lichtenberg Bahnhoff, the station for trains to Prague, which is in former East Berlin. Work was being done everywhere and the sparkling ticket booths and telephone kiosks were obvious signs of reunification change.

I said goodbye to Maria, boarded my train, and waved to her as it began to move off. Then I began a search for a seat. It was packed full of Inter-railers. You could hardly squeeze through the corridors for young travellers with rucksacks. I wandered through second-class, could not find space, so went to find somewhere in first class. Nearly all compartments there were empty. The train was made up of an extraordinary variety of carriages — Czech, Austrian, German and Russian (this one looked particularly uncomfortable). I found an empty compartment in a first-class German carriage, put my case in the luggage rack (I prefer to take a tiny suitcase on Inter-rail trips as they stop you being categorised as a budget traveller), sat down, slid the seat out to extend it, took off my shoes and put my feet up on the opposite seat. I took in a deep breath and dozed off.

I must have been asleep for only half an hour before the door crashed open and a ferocious, middle-aged woman burst into the compartment demanding my ticket. I showed her my Inter-rail pass and she flew into a rage. I could not understand a word (I think she was Czech) but she was obviously saying that as I did not possess a first-class ticket I was not entitled to sit there.

'Yes, I know,' I said. 'I pay for seat.' But she wasn't interested. Like a referee sending a player off the field she pointed to the second-class compartments. I pulled 20 marks from my pocket but that sent her into an even greater rage. There was no way that she was going to let me stay in first class so I trooped back to second class and eventually found some space by a toilet.

I had four smelly hours of further travelling. I didn't sleep a wink, but at least the night was not boring. For the first few minutes I tuned in to a strange conversation that an American boy was having with an elderly Czech lady, in very broken English, about the frequency of train crashes in Czechoslovakia. 'Big disaster, Prague,' she said. 'Big boom, Bratislava.'

'That's comforting,' I thought. 'It will be great when I have to be rescued from the toilet.'

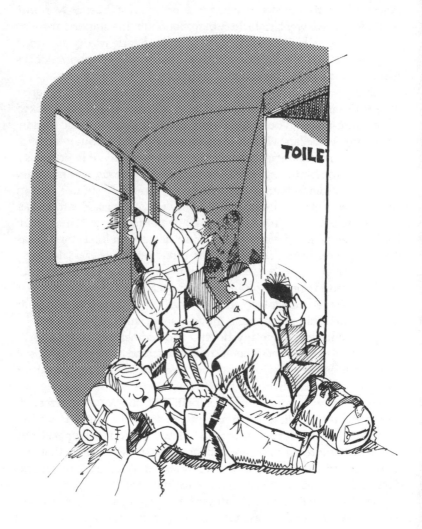

At three in the morning we crossed the border. First German officials and then their Czech counterparts came aboard. Two Czech boys were led off the train protesting after customs men inspected their luggage and found it stuffed full of computer games. Shortly before Prague there was more drama when we stopped at a small station and an American boy ran through the carriage shrieking that his rucksack had been stolen. I had witnessed the same problem on an Inter-rail trip before – the lad had left it in his compartment while he made a visit to the loo (I had slid aside to let him in). Someone had seen it then jumped off the train with it. 'My passport, my money, my tickets, my camera. That pack contained everything I own and I'm not going back to Chicago 'til Christmas.'

We arrived in Prague at 6 a.m., which gave me two hours before I took the train to Vienna. A queue of taxis was already at the station. I jumped in one. 'Wenceslas Square please, then a quick city tour and the station for Vienna.'

'Thirty dollars,' said the driver.

'You must be joking.'

'Okay, 20.'

'No,' I said firmly.

'Fifteen,' he suggested.

'Look,' I said stubbornly, 'I can give you eight and nothing more.'

'Ten, ' he replied.

'Forget it,' I said and got out of the car.

He shouted to me: 'You got marks?'

'Yes,' I said, thinking to myself, 'and you're not bloody having any.'

'You give me 15 marks, okay?' I did a quick calculation. It seemed to be less than 10 dollars, although after a night by a Czechoslovakian train toilet, it was too early in the morning to be sure. I was too tired to haggle more anyway.

'Fine,' I said and jumped back in the car.

The poor driver did more than he had expected to earn his money. We drove first to Wenceslas Square where I got him to take photos of me standing by the statue of St Wenceslas – it was covered in flowers commemorating the 1989 democracy demonstrations. Then we drove round the city stopping at landmarks where he photographed me 20 more times. I thought Prague was beautiful but the driver must have thought me just a vain western tourist. We drove to the station for my connection to Vienna where I gave him two ten-mark notes. As usual, I had only haggled on principle.

The journey to Vienna took six hours and during the trip I met a friendly Hungarian family (the two children spoke some English and acted as interpreters) and chatted with the refreshments-trolley man. He was Austrian and, because he spent his time travelling on European trains, had a bagful of different currencies. After ordering a drink I found I had no Austrian schillings. 'No problem,' he said and we did a deal. He took my German marks and gave me schillings. Then when I said I was going to Italy he swopped marks for Italian lire. He gave me a bad rate, of course, but I thought it a useful ruse and he told me that refreshments-trolley men changed money on trains all the time. 'Exchange – make money. Necessary for the job.'

When we reached Franz Josefs Bahnhoff I shut my suitcase in a luggage locker and took a bus to the city centre. First stop was the Hofburg, the old Imperial Winter Palace which is home to the Spanish riding school and Viennese Boys' Choir. Unfortunately neither was performing. Notices said the horses were touring and the boys were on their summer holidays.

Vienna was elegant but I had just hours before my Venice train so I used the time to look at Freud's and Mozart's houses, visit the Prater fun-fair (and see the Ferris Wheel which appeared in Orson Welles's film *The Third Man*) and finally do a city-circuit on a tram (which is incidentally a great way to see the 'Ring', the innermost district of Vienna – trams go around it continually).

For my overnight journey to Venice I decided to indulge myself and at Sudbahnhoff, the station for trains to Italy, I reserved a bed on the sleeper-train. It cost £35 which I thought expensive considering I had to share the compartment. My companion was an Austrian businessman. At first he looked cool and urbane, but when we got into our beds my opinion very quickly changed. I was exhausted but could not relax because of his endless belching and farting. He also managed to snore non-stop too. I put in my ear-plugs, turned the air-conditioning up to maximum and hours later eventually fell asleep.

When we arrived in Venice I was bleary-eyed and Venice is not a good city to be bleary-eyed in. I felt a tug on my camera bag and turned round to see a man with his hands behind his back, standing behind me smiling nervously. Even at eight in the morning the centre was swarming with people. I took a Vaporetto to St Mark's, ordered a coffee in a café, and was promptly charged the equivalent of six pounds. That took nearly all the lire I had swopped on the train, so I had to wait for a bank to open, then queue up to cash a sterling traveller's cheque.

In the currency exchange queue I met two Inter-railers, Andy and Sarah from Glasgow. They had spent a month visiting all the places that I had briefly seen in three days. Neither watched 'The Travel Show'. 'What a job!' said Andy, after asking about my trip. 'Do you travel first class everywhere?'

We progressed to a café where we all talked so much that I missed my Paris connection. That meant another overnight journey and I was not enthralled by the prospect. At the station I tried to upgrade to first-class and pay the price difference with my credit card. But they told me everything was booked. All they had was a bunk in a second-class couchette.

This was similar to the Austrian sleeper except that instead of sharing a compartment with one person, you shared it with five others. It was less than half the price so I shouldn't have expected much but when I found my compartment, I was pleasantly surprised to find it already occupied by a pretty French girl. Within minutes the other passengers arrived – two French teenage boys and two Italian men in their forties. When bedtime came, the Italians stared and waited for the girl to start undressing. But with great French female aplomb she just ignored them, took off her jacket and shoes and climbed up the steps to her bunk. One of the Italians flicked off the lights and soon began to burble in his sleep. 'Gabriella! Gabriella!' he moaned. It was going to be another bad night.

To my surprise I slept well. I was so tired that nothing could have stopped me. We arrived at the Gare de Lyon in Paris at 7.00 am, I took the Metro to the Gare du Nord and got on the next boat train to Calais. After an uneventful cross-channel trip I arrived at Victoria at two in the afternoon. I took a taxi to the Broadcasting House mail office to deliver my films from the trip (they always freighted them to BBC North for me) and returned to Walthamstow. I spent a night in my own bed and went up to Manchester the next day. I know it sounds a typical British Rail-knocking cliché but having ridden on trains all over Europe this was one of the worst. Maybe I was unlucky but it was dirty, uncomfortable, out of date and late. 'British Rail apologises for the standard of this train on our 9 a.m. service to Manchester,' said a voice. 'But this is a 25-year-old piece of rolling stock, due to be de-railed next month, which was only scheduled for this journey at short notice. I hope you all bear with us and we look forward to seeing you on British Rail again soon.'

They saw me again that night when I finally completed my rail journeys for the week and went back to London and then to Gatwick by train before taking a plane to my next destination.

CHAPTER EIGHTEEN

An Austrian Treat

A week on European trains was not my favourite assignment but it was almost worth the hassle for a wonderful trip given to me for the final programme in the series. 'You've had a busy summer,' said Penny. 'So this week we're giving you a treat. We're sending you to the spa town of Baden near Vienna where you're going to stay in a health farm. It's attached to an elegant hotel and you're on the three-day anti-stress package. Try to calm down, have a relaxing time and come back refreshed to us next week.'

I was delighted. I had always fancied visiting a health farm and could not think of a better way to finish a hectic summer for 'The Travel Show'.

After the programme I picked up my instruction sheet from the office and saw to my astonishment that this really was to be a relaxing trip — I was to be met at Vienna airport by a chauffeur who would then drive me in a limousine to my luxurious Baden hotel. Luckily I had time to go home and pack a change of clothes. I needed a few smart things as I wasn't going to be sleeping beside smelly train toilets this week.

After flying to Vienna I passed through immigration and customs and looked out into a sea of people for my chauffeur. A youngish man with blonde hair, dressed in a smart suit, was holding up a sign marked 'BBC'. I approached him and went to shake his hand.

'Pleased to meet you,' said the man. 'Elmar Derkitsch. Delighted. May I carry your bag? The car is very near — just two minutes over here.' He picked up my suitcase, led me towards the car-park and pointed to a large green Mercedes. With great servility he loaded my suitcase and camera bags into the boot, then opened a door of the car. It was a front door which I thought presumptuous – I might have preferred a back seat.

'So welcome to Vienna,' he said, as we drove off.

'Thank you,' I replied. 'How far away's the hotel?'

'Not far at all. We'll have you there in less than half an hour?'

'Great,' I said, then shut my eyes and tried to doze off.

'Mr. Collins,' interrupted the chauffeur. 'Would you care to make a diversion into Vienna? A quick look at some of the sights?'

'No thanks,' I replied. 'Let's just get to the hotel.' I shut my eyes again and tried to sleep.

Two minutes later he piped up once more. 'So did you have a good journey Mr Collins? Very tiring I suppose.'

'Fine actually. Had plenty worse.' I made no attempt at conversation.

'So your programme is called 'The Travel Show'. You are a presenter on the programme?'

'Yes.'

'And you produce your reports yourself?'

'Yes.'

'And what about a film crew? Will you use some people in Vienna or will the BBC send a team?'

'No. I just use a stills camera. I do everything myself.'

'So you have no moving film?'

'Only still pictures.'

'How interesting.'

'Yes.'

'Have you ever been on a health programme before?'

'No.'

'Well, you will enjoy this one, I can assure you. The Hotel Sauerhoff has excellent facilities and a really very professional team.'

'Good.'

'Oh yes, Mr Collins, you will enjoy your time with us here. I promise you will leave a different man.'

'Thanks.'

'So do you have any special dietary requirements for this week? The regime is not strict but if you wish, you may take what the hotel calls its special "vitall menu". This is low-calorie and also very healthy.'

'I'll talk to the people at the hotel.'

'As you wish, Mr Collins. I just thought you might like to inform me now. I can give any information you require.'

'That's very kind but I'll wait until I meet the hotel manager.'

The chauffeur then smiled, took in a deep breath, put his foot down hard on the accelerator, overtook all the cars in front of him and, cruising at 140 kilometres an hour towards Baden bei Wein, turned to me and said, 'Mr Collins. Did they not tell you? I am the Hotel Sauerhoff manager.'

'Are you?' I asked, horrified. I gave an ingratiating smile. 'Nobody told me. I thought you were... you know... just the chauffeur.'

'I am young for a hotel manager. I was food and beverages manager at the Intercontinental in Hamburg when I was only 25. Then I became sous-directeur at a hotel on the Canary Islands and manager at the Sauerhoff at 32. But you too are young to have such an important job with the BBC. Did you start off as a reporter?'

'Sort of,' I said. 'I started as hitch-hiking correspondent.'

'Excellent,' he replied. 'Anyway, I am sorry for the misunderstanding. Maybe we should start again... Welcome to Vienna. We have a very nice room reserved for you and remember that if there is anything at all you require, please do not hesitate to ask.'

'Thank you,' I said.

When we reached the hotel I saw to my suitcase myself. Mr Derkitsch rushed behind the desk to find my key, presented me with an information package which included the anti-stress programme timetable, led me to my room, told me to have a very pleasant stay, and then breezed back to his office.

I sat on the bed and looked at the timetable. There was a range of non-stop treatments and activities. I hardly had a daytime minute free. It certainly didn't look relaxing. I suddenly felt like I'd gone back to school.

The following morning I went for my first treatment — a *kneipp*. I did not have a clue what this was, and as an information sheet had suggested I didn't get fully dressed, I sat on a chair in my white hotel dressing-gown, picked up a German copy of *Vogue* and waited for an attendant.

'Mr Collins,' called a voice. A young girl in a white coat beckoned me into a large shower room. 'So, Mr Collins, welcome to the anti-stress programme. Please take off your dressing-gown and I will spray your legs with cold water. This treatment helps the circulation.'

I obediently removed my gown, stood facing the wall in my boxer shorts and the girl sprayed the calves of my legs. 'Very good, Mr Collins. And now a little hot...' She made the water hot then cold again.

After alternating the temperature several times she said, 'Good. Now back to bed for 10 minutes and please make sure you put on warm socks. This keeps your legs' temperature stable.'

'Right,' I said, puzzled. I was beginning to feel that I was in hospital. I put on my dressing-gown and retired back to bed but after 10 minutes I jumped out, had a shower, dressed and went for breakfast.

'Are you on the vitall menu sir?' said the waiter.

'No,' I replied. 'So could I have the full fry-up please.'

After sausage, egg, bacon, strong coffee, orange juice and toast, it was back to my room, back into my dressing-gown and back along the corridor to the treatment rooms. My next treatments were a manicure then a pedicure. Another young girl in a white coat trimmed my finger nails and then had a go at my feet.

Petra was very pleasant and as she gently cut my nails I began to feel relaxed. But the minute she finished my left foot's little toe the treatment abruptly ended. 'Okay, Mr Collins, swimming time now for you please.'

She showed me to the pool which was set in a Roman-style bath house. I did a few lengths then got out.

Andrei, the masseur, was next on my timetable. A large, smiling chap of about 30 dressed in spotlessly white trousers, shoes and T-shirt appeared quietly at the poolside and led me into a small room with a wooden bed and anatomical drawings on the walls. 'So today we have the all-over-body-massage and tomorrow we have the *shiatsu*. Okay?'

'Fine,' I said.

'So, lie on the bed please, Mr Collins.' I got on the bed, slid off my dressing-gown and Andrei went to work on my back. He put some oil on his hands and started gently rubbing my muscles. Tension seemed to drain from them immediately. Within minutes I felt drowsy.

'That feels great,' I said. 'How long did it take you to train?'

'Not long,' he replied. 'Three years ago I was a customs officer.'

'Really?' I said sleepily. This man had been wasted in customs.

Andrei gave me 45 minutes of deliciously soothing, tension-relieving massage. There was nothing sensual in it – the treatment was just wonderfully relaxing. Afterwards I didn't want to get up. 'So... finish,' he said. I felt like bribing him not to stop. 'You have lunch. I see you tomorrow for *shiatsu*.' I returned to my room, put on my clothes, went to the hotel restaurant and joined another guest at her table. We talked about massage all through lunch.

The afternoon started with a herbal bath. Petra ran it, threw some potions from different coloured jars into the water and told me to get in. It was the first bath I had ever had in my swimming trunks. 'See you in 15 minutes,' she said.

Quarter of an hour later she came back with some beautifully fragrant towels. I got out of the bath and she wrapped me up in all of them. 'Now we give you nice facial treatment.' I was allowed to get dry and led into another room where the beautician was waiting to pamper me with creams.

The day ended with yoga. It was a sunny afternoon so I went out on to the grassy courtyard with Petra. I twirled my head around in the sun, sat in a poor imitation of the lotus position for 10 minutes, then it was back to my room, for reading and TV followed by dinner and an early night in bed. I hadn't felt so calm for months.

The next day began with another *kneipp* – leg spraying first – cold/hot; cold/hot – then back to bed in my socks. After breakfast it was time for 'slide styling'. I didn't understand this treatment at all. I sat on a bed and my legs were encased in what looked like huge astronauts' boots. Tubes were attached to them, a machine was switched on and I was told to wait for 15 minutes. I couldn't go anywhere anyway. 'I come back very soon,' promised Petra. Unfortunately she forgot about me and the boots started vibrating furiously. According to the spa literature these were supposed to benefit the lymph glands and reduce the fluid in my legs. When Petra returned and turned the machine off they didn't look any different.

After coffee it was gymnastics in the garden – gentle stretching exercises – then a light outdoor lunch. The afternoon was enjoyable. Reflexology – a lady played with the pressure points on my feet relating to the different organs in my body – then Andrei gave me a glorious *shiatsu* massage. The day ended with a sauna. Dinner was steak, and apple strudel with cream followed by another early night. Time passed imperceptibly, I really had wound down. The following day was, sadly, to be my last.

It started with the usual *kneipp* then breakfast and an oxygen bath (this was like a jacuzzi – bubbles were blown into the water). Then I went for an acupressure massage with Andrei. That was as wonderful as the other two – except for this he concentrated on muscular pressure points, kneading my muscles like dough – and after lunch I went for the anti-stress programme's final massage. This was to be a 'brush and herbal oil wrap', with Barbara, the girl who usually gave the *kneipp*.

She beckoned me into a cubicle, shut the door and said; 'Okay, Mr Collins, now take off your clothes.'

'I'm sorry?'

'Take off all your clothes.'

She stared and waited. I undid my dressing-gown, put it on the bed while she waited for me to remove my boxer shorts. I turned round modestly, slid them off and quickly wrapped a towel round my waist. 'No towel,' she said. 'Take it off please, Mr Collins.' Barbara was no more than a teenager and was ordering me to stand stripped in front of her.

'But I'm British,' I said. 'We always keep our towels on.'

'Mr Coll-ins...' She was getting bored. I dropped the towel, she pushed me on the bed, said: *'Das ist nor-mal'* and started to rub my bottom with a brush. It felt like old horse hair. I winced and laughed – it tickled none the less. 'Yes, Mr Collins?' she asked.

'Nothing. It's just that the brush is a little ticklish.'

'Ticklish?'

'Yes, the bristles are also hard on my bottom.'

'Ah, so... this is good quality brush.' She continued to rub my bottom then my legs. I felt like a horse that was about to be saddled. But the pounding suddenly stopped and tiny droplets of hot oil began to land on my body. Barbara rubbed them into my skin, spreading the warmth over my back. She worked her way down to my legs, putting oil on my bottom en route. When she reached my feet I started giggling. 'Mr Collins...,' she said. Barbara was getting angry. I shut my eyes and thought of England.

When the treatment was finished she wrapped me up in towels and admitted that the 'brush massage and herbal oil wrap' often caused problems with male clients. But not with the liberated Austrian men, or even most other Europeans. It was the British and Americans who experienced the worst embarrassment undressing. Barbara could not understand the fuss.

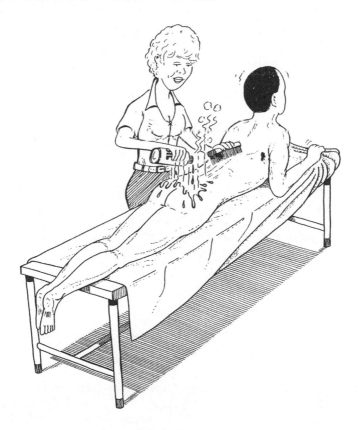

Talking to Petra and the beautician later I also learnt that health-farm trips were increasingly popular with male clients and that the favourite treatment for most of them was not the massage (either by Andrei or Barbara) but the facial. 'They love it,' said Petra. 'Most have never had one before and once they come here they promise they'll soon have another one.'

'Waxing is also popular,' said the beautician. 'You would be surprised at the number of men who want hairs from their back, shoulders or chests removed. It's becoming more popular all the time.'

After three days of pummelling and pounding I went home refreshed and un-stressed but the few hairs on my chest remained intact.

CHAPTER NINETEEN

The Trip of a Lifetime

I can thoroughly recommend a health farm to anyone who wants to be pampered – but that was not my best trip for 'The Travel Show'. This had me so stunned when Penny gave it to me on the programme that my response was quite unbroadcastable – I thought the whole thing was a joke.

'Now Matthew... you're off to America... you're going to New York... but this time you're travelling in style... you're sailing there on the QE2, leaving Southampton this evening. You arrive in New York in five days' time... so you will need a different wardrobe – a dinner suit... But that's not all – in order to catch the programme next week you'll be coming back to Britain on Concorde. There are no catches whatsoever. Have an absolutely fabulous time and tell us all about it next week.'

I simply could not believe it. This was another end of series treat but, after so many low-budget trips, I had never dreamed of anything so fantastic. When the researcher gave me my tickets at the end of my programme my hands were trembling. 'You'll have to rush,' she said. 'Your flight from Manchester to Gatwick leaves in half an hour and then you've got to collect a hire-car and drive to Southampton.'

I grabbed the dinner suit, specially hired from Moss Bros. The wardrobe man thrust a case of other smart clothes in my hand, and I jumped into the taxi waiting in front of BBC North. I made it on to the plane with seconds to spare and, when we were airborne, started talking to one of the stewardesses. 'I hope they've given you something nice this week,' she said. 'Because you've had some rotten ones in the past.'

'Well, I certainly can't complain,' I told her. 'I'm going on the QE2 to New York and then coming back to London on Concorde.'

'Wonderful,' she said. 'When do you sail?'

'Tonight at 8 o'clock. And I've got to drive to Southampton from Gatwick.'

She sighed and looked doubtful. 'You could have trouble. We're going to be held in stack over London then you'll pick up the rush hour around Crawley. I would try the train if I were you.'

'But I haven't a clue about times. I don't suppose you know, do you?'

'No,' she said. 'But I'll see if the Captain can find out.'

She disappeared into the cockpit and came out a few minutes later. 'Well, he's been on his radio and done some research. There's one at five thirty that gets in at seven fifteen – you'll probably miss that. And then there's another at six that arrives at seven forty-five. Everyone thinks you should get that one. They all think driving would be crazy.'

When we finally landed at Gatwick (after circling London for what seemed like hours) the stewardess let me disembark first. Then she told the baggage handler that I was in a desperate hurry, and asked if he would allow me to locate my luggage in the plane. I dived into the hold, showed him my cases and he took them immediately to the carousel. I collected them in the terminal, ran to the BR station and the train arrived a few minutes later. I boarded it praying I would reach the ship on time.

At Southampton I took a taxi and asked the driver to drive as fast as possible. At the entrance to the docks I could see the QE2. She looked enormous, sleek and beautiful. I rushed through check-in and boarded her only minutes before the gang-plank was raised. 'You were lucky,' said an officer who then proceeded to tell me an apocryphal QE2 story: 'An American lady was late once. We had to sail without her and then she suddenly appeared at the dock side. A tug was sent to collect her, it brought her alongside us and then a rope-ladder was thrown down. But she got stuck half-way up and was too scared to climb any further.'

'So what happened?' I asked.

'A message was sent to an officer on the tug. He had a word with her but she still wouldn't move... So he bit her on the bottom...

that soon got the lady to the top.'

As we left Southampton and cruised into the Solent the scene looked like one from the history books. Most passengers on the ship stood on deck waving handkerchiefs and tiny boats swarmed all around us. The QE2 gave a blast on her foghorn and we sailed further out to the Atlantic.

After the day's excitement I didn't make it to dinner. The swell of the sea lulled me to sleep and I didn't wake until five next morning (it was actually 6 o'clock on my watch but one great thing about sailing west across the Atlantic is that each day lasts 25 hours as the clocks go back an hour every night). When I looked out of my porthole all I could see was sparkling blue ocean. There were some papers under my door – a copy of *Satellite News* (printed on board – it was full of news from Britain and the States) and a programme of the day's events. What did I fancy? Morning prayers with the Reverend Kelwyn Adams? A dance class? Handwriting analysis, shuffleboard, quoits or a game of golf? 'Breakfast first,' I decided.

Breakfast was my introduction to the luxury of the ship. As well as the waiters, there was a jam boy whose job it was just to put dollops of jam on diners' plates. I took a croissant and the rest of my first meal consisted of smoked salmon with scrambled eggs; kippers; sausage, bacon and beans; coffee; fresh orange juice and toast. After breakfast I went to one of the lectures. It was called: 'Yes, you have a book in you – how to write your memoirs' and was given by an elderly American. I wasn't inspired. Some of the older ladies in the audience fell asleep and I felt quite sorry for the lecturer. When he got on to how to photocopy your memoirs I left.

After the lecture I enrolled on a computer course. En route to the computer room I passed through the theatre bar. A young chap who looked like he'd just walked off Wall Street was lecturing about stocks and shares. The bar was packed. 'These are always popular,' said an elderly American, who told me he had been on the ship ten times.

The computer course was given by a young American from New Jersey called Dave. He was enthusiastic, energetic and an excellent teacher. Within minutes he had taught people who had never even touched a computer how to use many of the basic functions. At the end of the lecture I chatted to a Spanish couple – they had won the trip on a Spanish TV game show.

During the five days that it took to sail to New York I met the most eclectic range of people. Among them were a millionairess from Manhattan who spent six months a year on the ship (she told me she had been interviewed by Alan Whicker) and a miner and his wife from Yorkshire. One night I also met a Californian lawyer and his family.

He must have been nearly 60 and his wife about 25. She told me she was an actress. His two daughters were only slightly younger than her and each night the women appeared in different stunning outfits. As this was such a special trip 'The Travel Show' had given me a video for the first time. I thought this glamorous group would look great on camera so I approached their table, said I was doing a report for BBC television and asked if I could take a few shots of them.

'Sure,' said the man and asked me to join them for dinner. I said I only needed a few seconds but he told me to sit down and ordered more wine. I took a sip – it was the most delicious red wine I had ever tasted. The man refilled my glass. The main course arrived – it was duck. I finished my wine again and the man continued to pour me more glasses. At the end of the meal the wine bill arrived. Out of the corner of my eye I managed to see the price. It was $300 – $150 a bottle and I had consumed most of it.

'So where's your film crew?' said the man sleepily. 'We'd better be getting off to bed.'

'Er, I don't have a film crew,' I said. 'I do all my filming myself.' I pulled the little camera out from my bag and the man's eyes nearly popped out of his head.

His wife and daughters looked uncomfortable. Maybe his wife had thought this would be her big break. 'Okay,' I said. 'I'll switch it on and when I count to 10, you act as naturally as possible. Talk amongst yourselves and try not to look at the camera.' None looked happy. I ran the video for two minutes, thanked them very much, and quickly left.

The next day I was chatting to an officer who told me that the American had been asking lots of questions about a man who said he worked for the BBC. 'Yes,' he said. 'He certainly wanted to know more about you. Apparently you'd been chatting to his daughters and knocking back his expensive vintage wine and he thought you might have been a conman. I suppose it's understandable. We do get all kinds on board.'

I avoided the lawyer after that and certainly didn't get to dance with his daughters. I did dance with the Captain's secretary though, and a retired Blackpool landlady who tried to make a trip on the QE2 each year.

Apart from finding passengers to be in my video and persuading others to take shots of me (I eventually met a photographer with the *Financial Times* who was extremely helpful) the main problem I had was making a choice from the huge range of on-board activities and entertainments. I wanted to see all the feature films (many had not been released in Britain) but also wanted to attend most lectures (the only one I was NOT interested in was called 'How to carve an all-American rooster weather-vane' — that was a little obscure for me). Then there was the swimming (in two different indoor pools as well as one outside — although that was quite chilly until the final days), the aerobics classes and of course the eating. You could spend the whole trip pigging out if you wanted. After a formal breakfast, you could have a buffet breakfast, morning coffee, a formal lunch, a buffet lunch, afternoon tea, dinner and finally a midnight buffet. The scenes at the midnight buffet were incredible. Huge ice-sculptures adorned big tables which looked as if they might buckle under the weight of all the food. There were huge joints of meat, exotic-looking dishes, whole salmon, prawns, vegetables and salads and wonderfully enticing desserts. Each night it looked like a medieval banquet. There was more than enough for everyone on board but many passengers still frantically loaded up their plates just in case things somehow ran out.

I arrived in New York feeling refreshed, relaxed and overweight. I hadn't managed to sit at the Captain's table but I had met him at a couple of cocktail parties. The night before our arrival he invited me on to the bridge for the next morning's sail up Manhattan. The man from the *Financial Times* filmed me against a backdrop of skyscrapers and just as I was about to disembark the Captain asked if I could take a small package back to Britain for his wife. He knew I was flying back on Concorde.

I only had a few hours in New York. I did a quick bus tour and then went to Kennedy Airport.

As I entered the First Class lounge I saw Concorde standing by the gate. Like all the other passengers I was very excited. We boarded the plane, the engines were started and, as we took off, the pilot gave a fascinating and terrifying commentary – he told us how fast we were going, how hot we were getting, how much fuel we were burning and by how much the aircraft metal was expanding. Then it was champagne all the way and, three and a half hours later, a safe landing at London's Heathrow. I was full of champagne but I still had the sense to think about the package from the Captain.

It was addressed to his wife but completely sealed and I didn't know what it contained. It had to be something innocent but I decided to declare it at customs. I told the officer I had been given it by the QE2 Captain. 'And you have no idea what's in it?' he asked.

'No,' I said.

He took off the outer brown wrappings and came to some white tissue paper. Inside was a sexy black négligé.

The customs man smiled and helped me to wrap it up again. It looked very scruffy so I wrote a little message: 'A million apologies but this package was opened by customs.'

'He'll never believe that,' I thought.

Sure enough he never did. Everything would have been fine had the QE2 experience not given me a taste for ships. The following winter I booked a Caribbean cruise on a different Cunard ship. When I boarded it I noticed that the Captain was the same one who had commanded the QE2 over the summer. I entered the restaurant on my first night for dinner and to my horror the maitre d' showed me to the large central table.

Finally the Captain arrived. He introduced the passengers to each other, then turning to me said: 'And does anyone know this chap here?'

'Oh no...' I thought.

'This is Matthew Collins. He works on a TV programme called "The Travel Show". Well, Matthew was on the *Queen* on a transatlantic crossing when I was in command in the summer. We got to know each other and, as he was returning immediately from

New York on Concorde, I gave him a package to take home. It was for my wife and contained a special present. Well, what did Matthew do? He sent it to her covered in packing tape and said it had been opened by customs.'

I went bright scarlet. The blood vessels in my cheeks almost burst. 'And what did Matthew find in the package?' he asked. 'A lovely little sexy black négligé...' There was silence for 10 seconds then a few people laughed. The Captain turned to me again. 'Now, Matthew, what are you drinking?'

'Red please, Captain. And don't give me any packages on this trip.'

[P.S. I should add that the Captain and I are now great friends. He even sent me a Christmas card last year (I trust he'll send me one this year too).]

[P.P.S. After hearing the tale of the American lady who missed the ship, had to take a tug boat and then had her bottom bitten to encourage her to climb up the rope-ladder, it entered my own collection of stories.

In 1994 I was guest lecturer on a Fred Olsen, cruise ship, the Black Prince. I told this tale to passengers during a morning lecture and, after going ashore that afternoon, arrived at the docks to find (to my horror) the ship slipping away gently to France.

The harbour master radioed for a tug boat and, after what seemed like hours, we pulled up alongside the Black Prince. Hundreds of passengers who'd heard my morning lecture were leaning over deck rails, laughing, taking pictures, and enjoying the spectacle of the experienced traveller (and on-board lecturer), standing shamefacedly on the tug boat. You guessed it — a rope ladder was then thrown down and I had to climb it to board.

For the rest of the cruise the comments never stopped: 'How's your bottom Matthew? Let's see the teeth-marks.' My professional credibility was lost.]

CHAPTER TWENTY

Alone With a Video Camera

In 1992 the new 'Travel Show' producer decided that all my reports would henceforth be on video. I thought the idea was excellent. I was presented with equipment — a video camera, tripod, extension microphones, a TV monitor, batteries, chargers, a professional Walkman, headphones — and sent for some instruction with a cameraman. Then it was off to Montana, in the old Wild West, for a trip to a huge cattle ranch.

'My wife thinks I'm going through a mid-life crisis,' said Fred, a 40-year-old mechanic from New York.

'It's what I've always dreamed of,' said John, a 50-year-old lawyer from Boston.

'I just want to ride in open spaces,' said Peggy Sue, a 25-year-old secretary from San Francisco.

All of us were in a pick-up truck heading for the Pryor Mountains, where we were to be 'dude cowboys' for a week. This is the slightly insulting term that locals use for townies playing cowboy. A 'dude ranch' is a ranch specifically set up for tourists. But our one, the Dry Head, was different. This was a proper ranch and holiday-makers came here to work.

In true American style our first stop was for a shopping trip. We were dropped off at a cowboy outfitters in the small town of Billings and picked up 90 minutes later. Most of us had spent around $100 dollars each. I had a stetson and a pair of boots with spurs and the manager of the shop filmed me walking out in my gear.

Two and a half hours later, after a drive across bare tracks, we arrived at the Dry Head ranch.

'This is not what I expected,' said Fred. 'I didn't realise we'd be so isolated. And I expected we'd be staying in a ranch house. This is nothing more than a shack.'

It was true our accommodation was basic – little more than a log cabin with beds. I was sharing my 'shack' with John, a lawyer from Boston. 'Come on in,' he said. 'Welcome to our home for the week.'

Once John had taken the shots of me entering the shack (a procedure that took an hour) it was time for an evening snack then bed.

The next morning, after an all-American home-cooked breakfast (bacon and egg, pancakes with maple syrup, cereal, orange juice and coffee), the cowboys got ready for the first task of the day. This was known as 'wrangling' – rounding-up the horses. Only the professionals were allowed to do it. The horses were led towards the ranch house from the hills, herded into the corral and then allocated to the guests.

'Now what are we gonna do with that camera of yours, Matthew?' said Dale, the resident professional cowboy.

'I'll just ride with it and keep it round my neck,' I said.

'Well you be careful boy,' he said. 'Cause we're gonna be roundin' up some cattle and we wouldn't want you fallin' off amongst them.'

The first day was great fun. The Dry Head ranch consists of nearly 20,000 acres on which nearly 2,500 cattle graze. 'I can't believe I'm doing this,' said Fred. 'Rounding up the cattle on a horse. It's just like in the movies. I'm really being a cowboy for the week.'

I chased the cows, trying to hold the reins with my left hand and control the camera with my right. Later there was branding, tagging, vaccinating, and then a task that made most of the men wince. Small rubber bands were put around the male calves' tiny testicles. The cowboys assured us it was painless but it was with gritted teeth that I filmed a short sequence. The producer later said she could not use it.

The other duties of the week included mending the fences, looking for water (some nearby streams had dried up) and going for some very long rides. (We thought they were for fun but the real cowboys said that they were to inspect all the cattle on the ranch.)

After a week on a horse I had some very sore muscles and six hours of video to take back. A BBC editor had to sit through the lot. We edited the film and the result was a four-minute report.

Over the summer I became more efficient with my camera (sometimes I would return with only two hours of recordings) but, as usual, being alone created problems. One week I was sent to St Tropez to make a film about finding a summer beach job. Everything was going well until some nudists on one beach threatened to throw my camera in the sea. I had similar problems when I was sent to a Buddhist retreat near Lockerbie in Scotland — many people there refused to be filmed.

The trip most damaging to my camera was a visit to the annual British Balloon Fiesta. This is a meeting of balloonists from all over the country which takes place in Bristol every summer. Going up in a balloon was one of the most graceful travelling experiences I have ever had (you just rise imperceptibly towards the sky and the almost total silence is only occasionally interrupted by ferocious blasts on the burner) but I did have to make sure my camera was well secured to the basket so that if the worst happened it would not fall out on someone's roof or head. I made three balloon flights but on the final one a sudden ferocious gust of wind blew us half a mile away from our chosen landing spot. We bounced uncontrollably along the bumpy ground screaming obscenities, not knowing how or where we would finally end up. We came to a stop in two different fields with the balloon in one, the basket in another and the attaching strings straddled across two hedges. My camera, to its credit, kept running all the time. Afterwards it needed a good service but at least I got some wonderful footage.

The best sequence I shot, however, was during a football cruise on the *Canberra*. This is a great idea and an increasingly popular type of holiday. The ship employs several ex-professional footballers (when I was there they had Alan Mullery, Norman Hunter and Ronnie Glavin) and they organise games and give interested passengers on-board coaching. Anyone who's ever followed football loves it. Playing with the pros is a privilege and when someone like Alan Mullery tells you 'Good shot' – not that he told ME that often – you feel incredibly inspired. The highlight of the cruise is always a match between a local port team and one made up from footballing passengers. We were cruising around Italy and our match was against the Trieste Port Authority XI.

As you can imagine, being Italians, their players took the game extremely seriously. Our team was mostly made up of people who had not played football for years – decades in some cases. Soon we were five-nil down. Unfortunately Alan Mullery wasn't playing but he bellowed his support from the sidelines. He didn't like the local tactics. 'They were always like this, the Italians,' he opined. 'I never liked playing them – they'd poke you in the eyes and hit you in the goolies and then try to make out they were innocent.'

As the match progressed, things became heated. I was on the pitch, playing and filming with my camera. *'Fuori! Fuori!'* boomed the referee, blowing his whistle when he noticed me. He ran straight at the camera and blew his whistle again, this time directly into the microphone. *'Fuori! Fuori!'*

'Oh refereee,' I said. 'I'm filming, I'm filming.'

'*Fuori! Fuori!*' he screamed.

I was about to continue my protests when a huge midfield player picked me up and threw me off the pitch. The camera was still recording while I was muttering something about Italians not only cheating in big internationals but even in small amateur games. It was great, dramatic footage but much of that was also edited out – we didn't want to create a Euro-incident.

My best memory of that year however, was of a trip I made with an Aborigine into the Australian Outback. What sticks in my mind are the extraordinary conversations we had and, in particular, the endearing questions he asked me.

I was in Australia for a 'Travel Show Guide' and my first stop was the remote Northern Territory. This is the least populated part of the country, where a quarter of the population are Aborigines, and I was on a Bill Harney tour.

Bill Harney is an Aborigine who takes tourists on trips to the Outback. There are hundreds of tours offered all over Australia (the country is so huge that it's the way that most tourists see things) but his are unique as they are operated on a such a personal scale. He takes the odd tourists into the bush but you don't just pay a visit you actually go to live there for two days. You sleep under the stars and Bill teaches you all about aboriginal life. He is the perfect teacher as he spent his early life here and comparing different cultures is fascinating. For 48 hours Bill and I were alone together and parts of our conversations went like this:

'So how are old are you then, Bill?' I asked him, when we were driving out together.

'To be honest Matt, I'm not sure. I could be 51 or I could be 71 so I reckon I'm somewhere in between. We didn't record birthdays in the bush. A policeman estimated mine when I applied for a driving licence 30 years ago.'

Later we were swimming in a billabong (a water hole). Tropical birds sang, cicadas clicked and a kangaroo bounced past in front of us.

'Got any billabongs in London?' he asked.

'We don't actually, Bill. But we do have a river – the Thames.'

'Got any crocs in the Thames, Matt?'

'No crocs in the Thames, Bill.'

'What about sharks then?' he asked.

'No sharks either,' I replied.

'Well, you must have some swordfish in it then.'

'No swordfish in it either, I'm afraid.'

Bill later asked if I wanted to go out hunting. He went to his truck to fetch his equipment and came back looking disappointed.

'I don't believe it,' he said. 'I've left my boomerang behind.'

We made do with a pre-cooked roast chicken and later had to light a fire with a match because all his firesticks were damp. But despite the occasional disappointment my time with him remained a great adventure.

'Matt, Matt, get your strides on quick,' he said to me early the following morning. 'And grab your video camera as there are two baby crocs hatching from their eggs.' I filmed the two emerging into life – they were only a few inches long. After the crocs he showed me some aboriginal rock paintings (many were over 40,000 years old) and talked about aboriginal customs.

In his tribe it had been traditional for the old men of a village to marry the young teenage girls. But it had also been traditional for elderly widows to marry the young teenage boys. 'It means two inexperienced people are never together,' he said. 'So it keeps tribal life stable and also means that everyone always has something to look forward to.'

The intense tropical heat and the endless fly and insect bites were the worst I had ever experienced but Bill's company made them more bearable. Unfortunately it was soon time to return to Katherine, the nearest town (after two days in the bush most tourists are ready to go back) but before we started our three-hour drive I did achieve one small ambition. Bill cut a branch off a tree (he chose one that had been hollowed out by termites). He shaped it up quickly and told me to blow through one end. In less than ten minutes I was getting a sound.

'There you go, Matt. Bet you didn't think you'd learn to play the didgeridoo while you were out here.'

'I certainly didn't, Bill,' I said. 'Just grab my camera and get a quick shot of me using it.'

* * *

In 1995, a few years after meeting Alan Mullery on the Canberra, I was walking past Fulham Football Club, probably the most beautifully located football ground in London – it's right on the Thames, next to a park and less than a mile from Putney Bridge.

Fulham's fortunes have taken a nose-dive since the days when Mullery played for them. But on a graffiti-covered wall, opposite the ground, you can still make out the large, white-paint-daubed words: 'ALAN MULLERY IS GOD!' (You can also still make out: 'JIMMY HILL – SATAN'S FRIEND.')

But anyway, I was passing the club looking at the message about Mullery, when I looked up and saw God himself.

'Hello, Matt. How're you doing?'

'Hello, Alan . . . I'm fine . . . How are you?' It was weird having just seen the graffiti on the wall.

I took a deep breath and told Mullery what I'd just read. 'It's funny how things change,' he said. 'I don't know how old that is. But these days the only kids who recognise me say: "Aren't you that old geezer who does football commentary on Sky."'

I was just happy that one of my football heroes remembered me.

CHAPTER TWENTY-ONE

The Wild Man of Beluga and The Kids at Echo Lake

In 1993, for my first trip of my tenth series of 'The Travel Show' I was sent all the way to Alaska. I was booked on a bus tour with other low-budget travellers but having heard about the numerous colourful characters who were attracted to America's last frontier, I wanted to meet some Alaskans.

'Well, you won't find anyone more exciting than Dennis Torrey,' said Carey Corrigan, a local TV weatherman, whose number I'd been given by a 'Travel Show' researcher. 'They call him the Wild Man of Beluga. He's lived out in the wilderness for over 20 years and he's a real Davy Crockett round here. He built his house himself, he lives off salmon, bear and moose and he's 20 miles from anybody else. He's only accessible by sea or air. Pay him a visit and tell him I sent you. You'll have a wonderful time.'

A few hours later I took off from Merril Airfield in Anchorage in a six-seater Spurnac Airlines light aircraft. My one-way ticket had cost $25 (although I had had to pay $3 extra for my rucksack) and I was accompanied by two men who were going to Beluga for the fishing. 'Well, I guess we'll make a night of it – catch a few salmon – then go to work in the morning.' They worked in the gas industry and were taking a 7 a.m flight back. After a 45 minute below-the-clouds flight we landed at the smallest airport I have ever seen – it consisted only of a dusty, gravel airstrip with a barrier, similar to those at railway level crossings, to stop cars straying on it. A single truck was there, waiting to meet us. 'How you doin? My name is Travis. I work for Dennis. He's sent me up here to meet you guys.' We clambered into the truck – and drove the 17 miles to the house.

'So you're the English reporter that Carey told me about. Welcome to Beluga, Matthew.' Dennis was a big middle-aged man – about five feet ten tall and very heavy. 'Come into the house, Matthew. I'll show you around.'

He had barely ordered one of his kids to make us some coffee when he started talking about poetry. 'Have you heard of an English poet called Robert Browning?'

'Of course,' I said.

'Well, he was my great, great grand-daddy,' said Dennis proudly. 'And do you know Westminster Abbey?'

'Sure.'

'Well, my great, great grand-daddy's buried there. I must get to England some day.' Dennis later told me that he didn't think that was very likely. He went to Ancorage only a few times a year and had been out of Alaska twice in 20 years.

'Well, this is the set-up,' he said, showing me his home. 'I built it all completely myself – from cutting down the trees for the house, to putting in the generators, digging the well and installing the septic tank. It's not kind of fancy here but we're comfortable.' He told me he had grown up on a farm in Michigan and trained as a toolmaker before deciding to move to Alaska. 'I used to read about all those old-timers as a kid – like Davy Crockett and Jim Bowie – and I dreamed of doing the same thing myself. I spent the first 10 years just living off the land – trapping animals to eat and selling their pelts – but the cost of fuel became so high (I have to have everything flown or shipped in so gas and diesal costs me nearly twice the normal price) that I had to start making some more money. That's when I started having tourists here for the fishing. You a fisherman, Matt? Well, you'll catch some big fish here. You like salmon? Well, we got Kings that are up to 80 pounds.'

We were still drinking our coffee when a man in a hunting jacket and baseball cap burst in. 'Dennis, you gotta help us. Ed's just shot a brown bear. He's a big son-of-a-bitch, man and he's down by the river. We need some help bringing him in.'

'Okay, guys,' said Dennis. 'You ever eaten bear, Matt? Cos you're gonna have yourself a bear dinner tomorrow.'

We all got into a pick-up truck – Dennis threw an enormous handgun on to the dashboard. 'Do you always take that with you?' I asked.

'Sure,' he said. 'Gotta have your gun round here. Only time I never took my gun, a moose charged at me and broke my neck.'

The bear had been shot near a river – flies were already swarming around it. It was huge but looked distressingly human. Travis and another man joined us and Dennis tied its legs to a long piece of timber which we all carried up the slope towards the truck. Less than an hour later the bear was hanging up in Dennis's garage and Ed and his brother were skinning it. I went to have a peek and felt sick. Without its skin the animal now looked even more human – like a great, limp hanging boxer, having his dignity as well as his skin stripped away.

I felt sure I wouldn't be able to eat it. 'Well, you don't know what you'll be missing Matt,' said Dennis. 'Cause I can tell you that bear is beautiful.' He then told me that his youngest child – his daughter – hadn't eaten beef until she was six. 'I bought her some hamburgers from the city. Do you know what she did, Matt? Hell, she spat everything out. She was only used to moose and bear meat.'

The next day the bear was carved up and half a leg was put aside for dinner. The rest of it was put in bags and frozen in one of Dennis's five big chest freezers that kept him continually supplied with food. 'Hell, you might not like it Matt, but this bear's gonna see us all through winter.' As well as plenty of vegetables from his garden he had frozen caribou, moose, partridge and salmon. 'Things get kinda difficult when there's 15 feet of snow out there. We have to think of food now.' He also reassured me that all the hunting and fishing he did was strictly controlled by the State.

The morning was spent cutting up trees which were going to be used to make more log cabins for tourists. His son cut them up with a chain-saw and then they were made into timber – Dennis even had his own sawmill. In the afternoon I went out with Dennis for a tour of the countryside on one of his motorbikes. Again he took his gun, strapping it on to the handlebars. While we were sitting by the river he saw me staring at it. 'You're kinda fascinated by my handgun, aren't you, Matt?' He told me it was a .44 Magnum – the same model Clint Eastwood had carried in his *Dirty Harry* films. 'You ever fired a handgun Matt?' I told him I hadn't. 'You want to?' I said yes. Dennis placed the Magnum in my hand. 'Just pull the trigger gently and aim for that barrel over there.' Bham! The bullet split the barrel in two. My ears rang and my hands felt all trembly. 'It'd blow your head off, that Matt.' Dennis then told me he had 33 guns altogether, including an 'elephant gun'.

'Why do you need one of those?' I asked. 'You don't get elephants in Alaska.'

'I just like to collect guns,' he said.

When the bear was finally pulled out of the oven, after five hours of cooking, it looked like a huge Sunday roast. Dennis carved for everyone and gave me my plate. 'Well, try your bear then, Matt,' he said. I placed a small piece on my fork and examined it. 'Well, go on boy,' he said. I raised the fork and the meat almost melted in my mouth. The bear tasted just like tender beef. 'Go help yourself Matt, 'cause there's plenty more.'

My next few days in Beluga were spent fishing. I went out with Larry, a friend of Dennis, and his family. Larry and his father had fly rods but to my surprise the rest of us were going to use salmon eggs for bait. 'I haven't been fishing for years,' said Helen, Larry's mother. 'I guess you guys should give me some tips.' But Helen didn't need any tips. Within an hour she had hooked a 40-lb salmon. 'Come on, come on,' she said as she hauled it in. 'Come on my beauty, come on now.' Larry's brother landed her catch in a large net.

'What are you going to do with it?' I asked her.

'We're gonna take it home and have a good old Montana barbecue.' But she didn't take it home to Montana. We ate the fish that evening. It was the end of my introduction to harsh Alaskan wilderness life and was the most delicious salmon I had ever tasted.

* * *

A few weeks later I was America-bound again – this time for a New York State children's summer camp.

I was travelling with BUNAC (British Universities North

American Club), an organisation which sends 4,500 British young people (aged 19 to 35 — many of them students) to work on 'self-financing working holidays' in American summer camps every year.

On the plane over I read their booklet. The advice it contained was amazingly forthright: 'Directors have complained to us that many European counsellors smell! Change frequently, shower at least once a day and use under-arm deodorants as the natives do.

'Americans do not find all British humour amusing. Avoid the "dirty" or sexual-innuendo type joke. Remember your dispatches home! Parents, girl/boyfriends worry when they don't hear from you.'

When I arrived at Echo Lake Camp, located in beautiful upstate countryside, a meeting was in progress. An American activity leader (or counsellor as they are known) had an announcement: 'I'm sorry to say that one of our British colleagues had to return home yesterday for personal reasons. I am sure we will all miss him but no doubt this camp will continue to run as efficiently as always . . . '

'What were his reasons?' I whispered to a British counsellor.

'His fiancé broke of their engagement.' he whispered back. 'He flew home to try and patch things up. It'll cost him a fortune — he'll have to pay his expenses himself.'

The deal that BUNAC offers (his side of which this poor Brit hadn't completed) is that they provide flights, set young Brits up with work on a summer camp (if they want to help with activities they must have arts or sports skills — alternatively they can work as kitchen or maintenance staff), give them around $500 spending money at the end of the season, then let them have six weeks free to travel round the States before they fly back to Britain.

Early returns I later learnt are a rarity — one or two per cent, according to BUNAC. Most of the Brits I soon met were gaining a hard-working but enjoyable insight into a unique aspect of American culture. The season was half-completed and already many were looking forward to their six weeks of travelling and, in particular, to staying with all the contacts they had made — many of them, apparently, wealthy.

'You should have seen it on parents' day,' said Mark, a 'maintenance man' (and second year Manchester economics undergraduate), whose main job was unblocking toilets. 'My

God! The cars — Cadillacs, Porsches, Jaguars, Rollers — one bloke even arrived by helicopter!'

Camp Echo Lake is owned by Amy and Morry Stein and was founded in 1946 by Amy's schoolteacher father. It has numerous sports pitches, well equipped arts and drama facilities and, of course, a lake for water-based activities. During the summer 450 youngsters (aged seven to 17) and 220 British and American employees live there. It costs $5,000 to send a child to the camp for eight weeks.

Amy informed me that a president of Harvard once called summer camps 'America's greatest contribution to education.' Morry preferred to call his 'an oasis of old-fashioned values in an increasingly consumerist world'.

I was soon struck by the traditional nature of camp life — as well as plenty of fresh air and healthy activities, there were no video games, smoking and drinking were banned (for children and staff — although in the evening some Brits went off to local bars) and bedtime was strictly enforced — 9.45 for teenagers, 9.30 for all younger children.

The standard of supervision was also high. Camps expect activities coaches to be experts in their field — many of the British were trainee sports teachers.

The youngsters however, were very much American kids of today. I was struck by nine-year-olds wearing designer clothes, 10-year-olds mentioning their lawyers, and 11-year-olds talking about stocks and shares.

'They are so much more confident and self-assured than British children,' said James, a former civil servant who had given up his job to teach tennis here.

'They're great,' said Shane the British golf teacher (who'd seen an advert for the post in a golf magazine) 'but they're always pestering you to admire their fancy shots. British children have usually played less golf so they pay more attention to what I say.'

Backstage in the kitchen some Brits just thought them little brats. 'I was wiping this kid's table,' said one, 'when he deliberately spilt some drink for me to wipe. "Come on," I said. "You wouldn't have me a home to do this." "No," said the lad, "We've got the maid to do that . . . ".'

Although the kitchen and maintenance staff didn't have the status of counsellors most of them seemed happy with their lot. 'I'd much rather spend 12 hours a day in the kitchen than 24 hours with the kids,' said another (many counsellors had responsibilities for the kids at night too).

'Yes,' I said to the lad. 'But do you still change frequently and wear under-arm deodorant as well?'

If you're interested in BUNAC's programmes, write to: British Universities North American Club, 16 Bowling Green Lane, London EC1R 0BD (Tel: 0171 251 3472).

PART FOUR

A Few Favourite Countries and Memories

CHAPTER TWENTY-TWO

France

Having worked on a travel programme for so long, I'm frequently asked the same question: 'What is your favourite country?'

It's a difficult one to answer as I love so many countries for different reasons. Most of my trips however, are to Europe and so these are a few memories from some of my favourite places.

Like many British people, I adore the food and landscape of France (I even like the people as well, although having lived there I have had some run-ins with them). I've had a love affair with the country since discovering the Côte d'Azur while at school. After endless family holidays in places like Bognor and Littlehampton I thought it was the most civilised, sophisticated place in the world. For three consecutive years I took the night train south and spent the summer camping, living as cheaply as possible.

Fired by my enthusiasm for France I ended up studying French at university. As part of the course, I spent my third year working as an *assistant d'anglais* – an assistant English teacher in a French middle school. The year got off to a bad start. When I arrived the headmaster said I was rather small. I was not sure of the significance of this until he nearly swooned when I told him I no longer played rugby. This was in a town near Toulouse, which I soon discovered was the rugby-playing centre of France (you even find churches here dedicated to 'Notre Dame du Rugby' – they're full of little statues of the baby Jesus handing a rugby ball to Mary). From that moment I was socially and professionally doomed. Then on my first day's teaching I made another *faux pas* and learnt an important language lesson.

I was half way through a class with the *troisième* pupils (14 and 15 year olds) when Chantal, the teacher, said I could leave early.

'Mathieu, you've done enough for your first day. Why not take the afternoon off?'

I thought it was a great idea, so she turned to the pupils who were conjugating verbs and said; 'Monsieur Collins is going to leave us now. He's just arrived from England so I think we should let him have a rest. Say goodbye to Monsieur Collins and we'll see him again tomorrow.'

'*Au revoir*, Monsieur Collins,' chanted all the pupils.

I said '*Au revoir*' and turned to give Chantal the *bisous*.

Planting kisses on a lady's cheeks every time you said hello and goodbye was a French custom I really liked (what I didn't like was that you also had to shake hands with the men, even if you see them all the time – men do it at work every morning, it takes ages but it has to be done). With the ladies the number of kisses varies according to the region and in this part of France it was two.

'*Au revoir*,' I said, seeking her cheek, but she chuckled and turned her face away.

'*Non, non.* I'm afraid I don't bother with that. I'm far too anglicised you see. I think it's a silly French custom.'

Believing I was saying 'So you don't kiss then, Chantal?' I said '*Alors, tu ne baises pas, Chantal?*'

The classroom cracked up. There were howls of laughter, giggling, tittering and hysterical repeats of what I'd said. Boys and girls banged on the desks and Chantal went a burning shade of red.

'*Calmez-vous!*' she shouted. '*Calmez-vous, je vous en prie!*' Then she took me outside to the corridor to explain what the pupils found so funny.

'You see Mathieu... un baiser is a noun. It means 'a kiss'. But *baiser*, the verb, is much stronger. What you actually said (and I will only very politely explain) was something like: 'So you don't BONK then Chantal?'... which is why all the kids have gone crazy. Don't worry about it though — you'll definitely be a hit with them now.'

I was a great hit with the kids — but although I loved the teaching there was not much to do at weekends. Luckily, as I had friends from my university teaching all over France, I also had plenty of people to visit. Frequently I would hitch-hike off to see them. Corsica was a favourite destination. I had a friend called Emma who was teaching in the capital, Ajaccio. One morning after returning to Marseille on the ferry I was hitch-hiking when a 2CV stopped. It was driven by a young trendy bloke who had a wicker basket on the back seat. He said he was going to Carcassonne, which was a good lift, so I jumped in and we started on our way.

Unfortunately for me, as I was in a hurry, he wanted to make frequent stops. We were on the smaller roads so he would find a pretty spot and take out his basket for a picnic. Each time he did so, he insisted that I share it with him. The first time he invited me to try a special cheese. 'It's a Corsican speciality,' he said. 'I managed to find it in a village in the north.'

He spread some on a piece of bread and handed it to me. It was strong-smelling stuff, pale yellow, drippy and full of strange little white bits. '*Qu'est-ce que c'est bon!*' he said, savouring a little piece himself. 'You like it? You want more?' I tried to say no but he didn't listen.

'What's it called, this cheese?' I asked.

'*Alors, c'est du fromage aux vers.*' I didn't know what *vers* meant but I nodded and said 'Oh right', so every time we stopped he insisted on giving me another portion. It got drippier and smellier and always contained the strange little white bits.

When I finally arrived back at school I went up to my room and looked in my dictionary to see what *vers* were. My heart sank when I read the entry: '*VER* (noun, masculine) worm/grub/maggot'. I had been eating maggot cheese! I later learnt that this is indeed a Corsican (and Sardinian) speciality.

During my year in France I wrote frequent letters to my family and once offered my mum a weekend in Paris. 'You fly to Charles de Gaulle Airport,' I said. 'I'll fix up the hotel, take you to restaurants, show you all the sights and pay for everything.' She was sceptical but eventually came. She let me know the day and time of her arrival and I hitch-hiked up to Paris three days early to arrange things.

I went to stay with a friend of mine, Kate, who lived in Pigalle, Paris' famous red-light district. We had such good fun and so much to talk about that I almost forgot my poor mother. On the afternoon of her arrival I looked at my watch: 'Oh my God,' I said. 'It's just gone four-thirty. Mum's plane touches down in 10 minutes.'

I ran to the Metro station, jumped on the train and arrived at the airport in a panic. I looked around the arrivals terminal and among all the sophisticated, expensively dressed women saw a lost-looking, innocent English lady.

'Mum!' I shouted.

'Thank goodness,' she said. 'For a moment I thought you might have forgotten me.'

I gave her a big kiss and picked up her bag. 'So where are we staying?' she asked.

'Oh... right...' I said. 'Well I haven't actually managed to book a hotel yet. Don't worry, we'll find one in a minute. But first we'll go to see my friend Kate. She's really nice and doesn't live far away.'

'But I've never met Kate,' she protested.

'Oh come on now mum. Relax, you're in Paris.'

I felt terrible. I was her eldest son. I had invited her over to see me and forgotten to book a hotel. I kept wondering what I should do.

When we arrived at Kate's I introduced her to mum. Kate was charming but mum was extremely embarrassed. 'Sorry about this Kate,' she said. 'That stupid son of mine hasn't booked a hotel.'

Kate made some tea and put on Radio 4 (reception is surprisingly good in Paris). She did her best to make mum feel at home and while they were chatting I slipped out to find a hotel. I popped round the corner and asked in the first one I came to. 'Do you have a room for the night?'

'*Mais oui*,' said the old Arab concierge.

'How much is it?' I asked.

'*Deux cents francs, Monsieur.*'

'Two hundred francs? Haven't you got anything cheaper?'

He told me he had something for 140 francs. I told him I would take it, bombed back to Kate's, burst into the flat smiling and told them I had found a lovely room. Mums' face showed obvious relief. I picked up her case, took it to the hotel and left them chatting. Then I came back and joined them for tea. At 7 o'clock we decided to go out for dinner together. The three of us left Kate's apartment and en route to a restaurant I popped my head into the hotel and asked the concierge if I could be back after midnight. '*Pas de problème, Monsieur,*' he said and added that he would still be at the desk.

Mum had a very decadent first night in Paris. We took her for a huge boozy meal and then to a jazz club until one in the morning. When she returned she was possibly a little tipsy. That was probably just as well because what happened next was extraordinary. I said '*Bonsoir*' to the concierge, picked up my key and went up to the room with mum. A few minutes later there was a knock at the door. It was the old concierge.

'Yes?' I said.

He peered round the door and started muttering in French. 'You know there's an extra charge if you bring back a tart?'

'I BEG your pardon,' I replied.

'You know it's 50 francs if you bring back a tart?'

'What ARE you talking about?' I demanded. 'This isn't a tart – it's my mother.'

He started sniggering and making foul suggestions to my mum. She sat like a demure lady on the bed. She smiled. She didn't know what he was talking about. 'Is everything all right, Matthew dear?'

'Yes mum,' I said. 'Everything's fine.'

'She's not bad,' said the concierge. 'Where did you find her?'

'Look,' I said firmly. 'This is ridiculous. That lady you are looking at is my mother. She's just arrived from Sunbury-on-Thames. She's not a bloody tart for God's sake.'

He carried on sniggering and asked me how much. I tried to slam the door in his face but then he turned rather nasty and said I had to pay the 50 francs. I stuck my hand in my pocket and gave it to him. He went away muttering to himself.

The following morning, when I told mother we were leaving, I explained about the misunderstanding.

'You're joking?' she said. 'My goodness – just wait until I tell your father.'

'Well he's not going to think I've looked after you very well is he?' I said.

'Oh I don't know. I'm sure he'll think it's quite funny.'

We checked-out of the seedy hotel and found another one far from Pigalle. It was full of Americans and extremely clean. Mum almost found it rather boring.

As there often is with my stories, there is also a follow-up to this one: the hotel incident was just the first in what turned out to be a very expensive weekend for mum. I ran out of cash and then had to borrow money from her to treat her the way I had promised. I swore that I would make amends and said that as soon as I started to earn some proper money I'd take her for a weekend at possibly the best hotel in Paris – the Crillon. (This was the one where I had met Peter Sellers as a courier.)

It was some time before I did earn proper money but a few years ago I kept my promise. Admittedly the Gulf War was on at the time and hotel bookings in Europe had plummeted. Luxurious places like the Crillon were half empty (in fact, especially the Crillon as it's located next to the US Embassy). So I phoned the hotel, we did a deal and I arranged a room for us both. Mum said it was worth the long wait.

CHAPTER TWENTY-THREE

Italy

My earliest memory of Italy is of arriving in Rome with someone from Liverpool whom I'll call Steve. I was 18 and he was 21 and we'd met up on the motorway hitch-hiking to the capital from Naples. This was my first foreign hitch-hiking trip and, having had some nerve-wracking experiences, I had been glad to find the company of someone older and bigger than me.

Our driver dropped us off in front of the Vatican. Thousands of people were flooding into St Peter's Square.

'What the hell's this?' said Steve. 'It's just like Anfield on a Saturday.'

An American told us that the Pope was about to give his weekly audience. He explained that the procedure was that he appeared in St Peter's Square, then drove round it in his famous Popemobile. 'So we're going to see the Pope?' said Steve. 'Oh that's brilliant... I'm a Catholic.'

We pushed our way into St Peter's Square, planted ourselves into a little space and waited. Suddenly the Pope appeared at the balcony of the Vatican palace. The crowd went wild. Nuns and priests cheered, mamas started screaming and papas threw their kids in the air. The Pope gave a blessing then retreated back inside the palace.

A few minutes later he reappeared, this time in front of us in his Popemobile. He circled the crowd and everybody tried to shake his hand. 'Look at this Matt – you can touch the Pope,' said Steve. 'I'm gonna shake the Pope's hand.'

Steve was huge – at least six foot four – so he had no trouble wading through the crowd. I followed in his wake pushing through the cheering nuns and priests. Suddenly the Pope was before us.

Steve thrust his arm out and, because it was longer than all the competition, his was the hand the Pope touched. He shook it for a second then the Pope continued on his way.

Steve turned to me. There was rapture all over his face. 'I can't believe it. I shook the Pope's hand. I SHOOK the bloody Pope's hand. That means it's sacred. I'm never gonna wash that hand again.'

We trooped out of the Vatican talking about religion with Steve promising he would go to church that Sunday. Unfortunately however, his spiritual fervour did not last long. He might have been an enthusiastic Catholic but he was also quite partial to stealing. Half an hour later he offered me a biscuit from a packet he said he'd stolen from the Vatican. He'd nicked it from a stall with the hand that had shaken the Pope's.

Steve and I soon parted after that. He was a kleptomaniac and the effect of my own Catholic background made it hard for me to enjoy his stolen goodies. We both went our own ways and I took a train back to France. But a couple of years later I was hitch-hiking again, this time with a girl-friend, Amanda.

Amanda had very blonde hair and hitching in Italy with her was a joy. Cars stopped frequently and at times we could almost choose the ones we wanted. But during the trip we had agreed on two rules: 1) that we would not take lifts from lorries and 2) that I would always sit in the front with the car driver.

One day however, we had been waiting in the countryside for nearly an hour when a Lancia stopped and a handsome young man offered us a lift. I opened the back door for Amanda but she said she was happy to sit in the front.

The driver tried to talk to her but Amanda spoke little Italian and when he ignored my conversational attempts I fell asleep in the back.

I woke with a start when Amanda suddenly pinched my leg hard. I jumped up to see her looking terrified – the driver had his hand up her skirt. She grimaced at me savagely, willing me to do something, so I coughed. The driver laughed, winked at her and stuck his tongue out. 'Oi!' I said feebly. The driver ignored me. 'Look!' I said limply. He laughed. 'Oi mate!' I shouted. 'Take your bloody hand off her leg!'

He removed it and Amanda started crying. 'Now let us out,' I said. 'Stop! Here! Now!'

We came to a screeching halt and Amanda and I jumped out. We grabbed our bags and he drove off. Amanda was trembling with fear. 'I've got to go to the loo,' she stuttered. 'I've go-got to go to the loo.'

We looked around. We'd been dumped on a tiny road with fields on either side. A few yards overhead was the motorway. Amanda ran off to find a hidden spot. Minutes later I heard sobbing cries.

A line of lorries on the motorway above had stopped to watch her answer nature's call. The drivers wolf-whistled, laughed, shouted and made gestures while Amanda crouched, fixed behind her bush. Tears were streaming down her face. 'I hate this country. I hate this country!' she wailed. She vowed never to come to Italy again.

We did, however, return, several times (Amanda wore trousers when we hitch-hiked after that) and once when we were Inter-railing we had another strange experience together.

We were travelling at night from southern Italy to Germany. The trains were packed but we found an empty compartment. We turned out the lights, spread ourselves lengthways on the seats, then both pretended to be fast asleep. For two hours, the doors were slid opened then slammed shut until we really did fall asleep.

When we awoke we found, to our horror, that we'd been robbed – only of a small bit of cash but our bags had been emptied and my wallet (which had been in my trouser pocket) was lying discarded on the floor. We informed the ticket inspector (who wearily took our details) but it was not until we got home, and by chance read a newspaper report, that the incident made us really feel nervous. Apparently, we learnt, gangs of thieves had been operating on various European trains. Their methods were freaky – they sprayed knock-out gas into the compartments and stole the occupants' belongings while they slept.

Describing all these events makes Italy sound like a country of perverts and thieves. That's not true at all and I have had many relaxing and uneventful trips there. But one of the most amusing was to Sardina where I was sent to stay with a local family for a week.

'You'll be met by Giovanni Riu at the airport,' said Penny. 'He'll take you to his home in the mountain village of Villa Nova where you'll stay with him and his family. He's a shepherd and we want you to join in with their day-to-day country life.'

I had my suspicions about Giovanni from the moment I met him at the airport. In his dark glasses and stripy blue T-shirt (with a packet of Marlboro stuffed into the breast pocket) he looked like the most worldly shepherd I had ever seen. He offered me a cigarette then proceeded to drive like a maniac, whistling at all the girls en route. It turned out that he wasn't a shepherd at all. 'I'm a taxi driver,' he said.

I thought the family was going to consist of his wife and kids but in fact it was his mother and father. Giovanni was 38 and still lived at home. 'Wouldn't you like your own place?' I asked.

'Why?' he said. 'No one could look after me like my mama does.'

His parents were both extremely kind. They weren't used to entertaining guests and his mother continually apologised for the modesty of their house, while serving me huge platefuls of food. '*Mangia, mangia,*' she kept saying. His father, who was about 70, ate little and spend most of his time sitting on a favourite chair in the dining room. During my stay I never once saw him take off his cap. He spoke a little English and every now and then, like an animated budgie, would suddenly utter his set phrases: 'Hello, Goodbye, God save the King.' He had learnt them in Tunbridge Wells as a prisoner of war in 1945.

There was only one inconvenience for Giovanni in living with his parents – his hobby was dating female tourists. Obviously he could not take them home so he usually entertained them in his car. There were bottles of Paco Robane after shave, wine glasses, a comb, and Richard Clayderman romantic music cassettes on the seats.

When I told him I was worried that he was not a shepherd, he said: '*Nessun problema – amici, pastori.*' It was true that he had friends who were mountain shepherds but many were business associates as well. Together they organised traditional rustic meals and, along with other tourists, Giovanni invited me to one.

It was actually a very enjoyable event. They sang songs and danced. The food was good – suckling pig, sausage and wine. But I resisted another local delicacy – *formaggio al vermi* (maggot cheese). To their astonishment, I told them that I had already sampled it.

The following day I also managed to do some shepherding. Giovanni woke me up at 5.30 and we went to meet a shepherd in the moutains. We rounded up his sheep and he invited me to milk them. I did the same thing with goats the next day. They were easier to milk – apparently their udders are bigger.

My trip was enjoyable but it wasn't a real shepherding experience. I did found out, however, that this is possible. An organisation called 'Agriturismo' based in the Oristano area of the island can fix tourists up for agricultural stays – with farmers, shepherds, horse-breeders or fishermen and for a 'Travel Show Guide' I spent a few days with a worker on a stud-farm. That was also an extremely enjoyable experience – and completely authentic.

CHAPTER TWENTY-FOUR

Spain

I have many amusing memories from numerous trips to Spain: of watching elderly ladies parade around a swimming pool with numbers attached to their wrists (I was a judge in a glamorous grannie competition in Benidorm); of a lady in Majorca complaining that she couldn't get 'Eastenders' on her own black-and-white portable TV (I was on assignment as a holiday rep); and of a former Desert Rat making a swastika from swimming-pool sun-beds to give a blatant message to the Germans (that stopped them keeping the sunbeds with their towels even when they were nowhere near the pool).

But these are just memories from the Costas – the big coastal strips that most tourists visiting Spain see.

My favourite parts of the country are those bits most British don't bother with. I love the Costa Brava but the part I adore is up in the north where the beaches weren't good enough for developers' exploitation. Cadaques (near the French border) is known as the 'St Tropez of Spain'. It's been full of poseurs ever since the artist, Salvador Dali, built an extraordinary house there (for some reason it has two huge white eggs on the roof). But although it gets crowded the atmosphere remains low-key and relaxed.

I'm not mad on the Costa del Sol (although Malaga which most people bypass is worth more than just a fleeting visit – there's nothing nicer than a sherry and some tapas in one of the old town's little bars) but further west, the Costa de la Luz is still authentically Spanish. (It's on the Atlantic coast which was considered too cold for northern Europeans and which is precisely why many Spanish love it.) Tarifa is one of best windsurfing resorts in the world and Cadiz has some of the wildest nightlife in Europe.

Many first-time visitors to the north-west coast find it hard to believe they're in Spain. The countryside is so green in parts that it looks more like Cornwall or Ireland.

I also love the Spanish cities. Madrid, Barcelona and Seville – all now European trendsetters – are favourite places of mine but no matter how much I adore Spain my memories of the country remain comic ones.

One enjoyable assignment for 'The Travel Show' was a riding trip to the Sierra Nevada. This is the range of mountains just north of the Mediterranean's Costa de Almeria. I spent a week with two other people riding cross-country through tiny whitewashed mountain villages. Every evening, when we arrived at our destination, children, dogs and chickens would all follow us. We would unsaddle the horses (usually in old stables below our small hotel), have a simple meal, then go to bed. The next morning, before the weather got too hot, we would set off on horseback again. It was a wonderful way of seeing an unchanged side of Spain and I enjoyed it so much that I forfeited a chance of a lift back to Malaga to spend an extra day on my horse.

There were no taxis in this area so there was only one thing to do when the trip finished – persuade a villager to take me. It was at least a two-hour drive so we negotiated a price and set off.

The drive turned out to be one of the most nightmarish trips I've ever done. Much of it was along the notorious N340, the busy highway that skirts the Costa del Sol which, before recent improvements, was one of Europe's most dangerous roads.

The old boy who was driving me put his foot down but we kept getting caught up in traffic. Eventually I arrived at the airport, five minutes before my departure time, convinced I had missed my flight home.

I paid the driver and ran to the check-in. Since Expo 92 Malaga Airport has been completely modernised but only a few years ago it was still predominantly a dusty old charter airport. When I arrived, all flights for the day seemed to have left. There was no sign of activity, the check-ins were deserted and the counter staff all seemed to have gone home.

I ran upstairs to the departure gates. There was hardly any activity there either. Cleaners were mopping the floor but most staff had disappeared. I ran through security – the post was deserted – and galloped past the unmanned passport control. I looked out of the departure hall window and saw a British charter plane outside. I ran to the gate, rushed down the steps and raced across the tarmac towards the aircraft. The door was still open so I sprinted up the steps and was greeted by an English stewardess. 'Going to Manchester? You're very lucky. We were about to close the doors.' She let me on board, took my ticket and showed me to one of the few vacant seats. I sat down on the plane, having reached it without passing through any kind of airport control.

My seat was by the window next to an elderly Irish nun. Shortly after take off she told me that she had just made her first visit to Torremolinos for over 35 years. She had been shocked at all the changes – but not so much at the loss of the once pretty little fishing village but at the type of tourist the town now attracted. 'Full of dreadful young British people,' she kept saying. 'Permanently drunk. And their language was atrocious. Effing and blinding. It was 'B' this and 'B' that. They had few other words to express themselves.'

I listened to her, as though in agreement, and kept saying respectfully 'Yes sister,' as she went on about the 'B's this and that.

The flight was uneventful. We took off, the evening meal was served and the passengers sat back and relaxed. The atmosphere was one of happy excitement as everyone looked forward to arriving home.

Suddenly the plane swerved terrifyingly to the left, dropping like a stone through the sky. Overhead lockers burst open. Hand luggage and duty-free rained down on the floor. Trays, cups and crockery went flying. Terrified passengers started screaming. I was dumbstruck. My heart missed a beat. The stewardesses rushed back to their seats. The plane righted itself (after what seemed like hours but was probably only seconds) but everyone nervously, frantically checked their seat-belts and waited for reassurance from the captain.

After two minutes a calm British voice came over the aircraft's P.A. 'Sorry about that,' said the Captain. 'We're presently flying at 35,000 feet and for some reason a plane flying in the opposite direction to us decided to descend to our altitude. Just to be on the safe side we made a move to the left. But everything's fine now, we're on our way home so if you'd like to accept a drink courtesy of the airline we'll have you on the ground in less than an hour. Sit back, relax, enjoy your flight and I'll talk to you all again soon.'

The passengers breathed in audible sighs of relief. I caught my breath and turned to the nun but she had gone red with embarrassment.

Not surprisingly. As the plane plummeted she had screamed out: *'BUGGER ME!!!'*

CHAPTER TWENTY-FIVE

Ireland

I have often found that extraordinary things happen when I go to Ireland. This was certainly so on my first visit. Despite all my travelling I had not even been there until a few years ago. Then 'The Travel Show' sent me to the beautiful west coast.

During the flight over, on a Sunday afternoon, I got chatting to a guy who offered me a lift from the airport into town. I accepted and when he dropped me off I went to find a local B & B.

At the third place I tried, an elderly man invited me in. He returned to the kitchen, where he had been playing with his toddler grandson, and told me there was a vacant room on the third floor. 'But I won't come wit you as I'm getting rather old so I'll be directing de traffic from down here... Top o' de stairs and den a right. You'll see number tree right in front of you.'

I found number three, threw my case on to the bed and went downstairs to tell him it was fine. His grandchild was playing with some small wooden bricks – circular, triangular and rectangular blocks, the ones young children have to hammer into a frame with cut-out shapes – but the child could not hit the blocks hard enough as he had his fingers wrapped around the hammer head. 'Now don't be stranglin' de hammer,' said the old man then showed his grandson how to hold it.

'What a beautiful phrase,' I thought. 'Stranglin' de hammer.' I told the old man I was going out briefly to buy a paper.

'Well make sure you get yourself a decent scandal sheet,' he said.

I had still only been in Ireland an hour. 'What a lyrical country,' I thought.

When I returned I let myself in, said hello to the old boy, who was still playing with his grandchild in the kitchen, and rushed up to my room to read the papers. I spread them all over my bed and was just about to settle down to a good Sunday read (before getting out my guide books to prepare my trip) when a gang of rowdy Irish girls arrived at the room next to mine. They were making an awful noise – shouting and laughing - and they seemed to be a fairly large group. They unlocked the door and entered, slamming it loudly behind them. The shouting, screaming and laughing continued, interspersed with banging on the walls. I couldn't imagine what they were doing.

I went back to my newspapers, concentrated on the Sunday gossip and tried to forget about them, but half an hour later there was more screaming, this time even louder than before. The door opened and slammed again, the shouting got worse and finally I decided to ask them to be quiet. I opened my door to find a group of girls gathered round the old man who was lying on the floor. All of them were sobbing. I asked what was wrong.

One girl, almost hysterical, informed me. 'Well, we were running a bath, and forgot about the water, and it started spilling out of the bath, and the man came up to turn it off, and the floor was wet, and he must have slipped, and he's fallen like this, and we just found him here, and he hasn't moved, and he doesn't look well, and Oh God what d'you think? He's gonna be all right isn't he? Oh God, please say he's gonna be all right. Please say he's gonna be all right.'

I bent down to look more closely at him. His eyes and mouth were open and his lips were blue. 'He's gonna be all right, isn't he?' said another of the girls. 'Oh do please say he's gonna be all right.'

'Well I don't know,' I said. 'I'm not a doctor.'

'Quick, quick,' said another girl. 'Someone fetch a doctor quick.'

'Yes, fetch a doctor,' said another.

'But where is a doctor?' said the youngest girl.

I put my ear to his chest. 'Hang on a minute,' I said quietly.

'Oh Jesus, Mary and Joseph, please say he's gonna be all right,' said the first girl. 'Holy Mary Mother of God, please don't say he's gonna die.'

'Well actually. . .' I said. I didn't want to disappoint them but this chap did not look healthy.

'Oh please,' said a girl, and all the others started wailing. 'Please, please, please...'

'Well actually,' I said.

'Oh no...'

'Well... to be honest...'

'No...'

'Well, to be quite frank... I'm afraid I think he's had it.'

'Oh God no, it can't be true.' And the rest of the group immediately started shrieking. 'There must be something you can do,' pleaded the first girl. 'Couldn't you try and give him the kiss of life?'

'I don't think there's any point,' I said. I pushed up his sleeve and touched his arm. It was cool and limp.

There was now uncontrollable wailing all around me. 'It wasn't our fault honestly. It wasn't our fault,' said the first girl. 'Maybe we should just quickly get a doctor.'

'All right then,' I suggested. 'You get a doctor and I'll go to try and find a priest.'

A few minutes later I was knocking at the door of a presbytery. A middle-aged man dressed in black with a white dog-collar opened it. 'Hello,' I said breathlessly, my heart beating madly. 'I'm staying at the guest house down the road and I think you should come as the gentleman who owns it has had a heart attack and I think he's very possibly passed away.'

'Oh, that old fella,' said the priest. 'Oh God yes — he's got a history of heart trouble. He'll be as dead as a dodo.' He put on his coat and hurried with me to the guest house. When we got there, the crowd round the body had grown bigger. Friends and other guests, including two Swedish girls from a room on the floor below, had arrived and were staring at the old man while a woman was leading the little boy out. The priest passed through the crowd, took the man's hand, and said some prayers. The old fellow's wife arrived. Someone tried to explain to her what had happened but she did not listen. She shut his eyes, kissed his cheek, said 'Goodbye my love' and retreated in shock, comforted by two elderly female neighbours. A doctor appeared, announced officially that the old man was dead and told everyone around him to go back home.

The Swedish girls and I did not have a home to go to so we

returned to our rooms. Then we went to the pub. Over a couple of pints of Guinness we talked about the man, the Irish girls and Ireland. This was also their first visit. 'It is a strange country,' said one.

'What a thing to happen,' said the other. 'Will we have to find another place to stay in?'

'I don't know,' I said. 'I don't think we'll be able to stay there.'

When we returned to the guest house there was a small, black-edged, notice pinned to the door. In neat handwriting were the words: 'Due to the recent death of my husband this establishment will be closed for Bed and Breakfast until further notice.'

'Well, that's it,' I said. 'We'll definitely have to find somewhere else.' I knocked on the door and asked the lady who answered it (whom I had not seen before) if we were expected to check out of our rooms.

'No, not at all,' she said. 'Not if you're already booked in. We couldn't kick you out on the streets. We might be a little disorganised but breakfast will be served in the morning.'

We headed up to our rooms. I said goodbye to the Swedish girls and continued up the stairs to the third floor. There was a small group in the room next to mine. I popped my head inside and to my horror saw the old man lying in an open coffin surrounded by people paying their respects. To add to the shock one man told me that the old boy would be there until at least the following morning. I did not know what to think or do. Up until an hour before I had never even seen a dead body and now I had to spend the night next to one. I went back down to the Swedish girls and asked them to return to the pub with me. All the talk there was of the old man. We each had two more pints of Guinness and then went for something to eat.

Two hours later, and suitably fortified, we returned to the guest house. It was now 10 p.m. 'Sleep well,' said one Swedish girl.

'Yes, good luck,' said the other.

I entered my room, opening and closing the door quietly. Then I put on the latch and barricaded the door with a chest of drawers and a chair. I hurriedly got undressed, brushed my teeth, put on my pyjamas and crawled into bed pulling the blankets up over my head. After four pints of Guinness, then lagers in the restaurant, I was asleep in seconds.

But just over an hour later I was awake once again. Voices were coming through the wall. My head felt fuzzy and, for a moment, I forgot where I was. Then I remembered and, in the darkness with the voices getting louder, I stuffed a couple of ear-plugs into my ears, pulled the blankets back up over my head, shut my eyes and tried to sleep again. But it was no good. The more I tried to concentrate on sleeping the more I found it impossible to relax. My heart kept beating faster and eventually I became so tense that I jumped out of bed, switched on the light, pulled out my ear-plugs and got dressed. There was now such a commotion coming from the room next door that I thought there was a party going on. I opened my own door and quietly looked around – *there was* a party going on.

The room was full. Half the people who had been in the pub earlier were there plus plenty of others – assorted relatives I assumed. Everyone had a glass in their hand and was toasting the body, saying what a grand man he'd been. 'Come on in,' said one man when he saw me loitering outside. Then he poured me a stout and proceeded to tell a story about the deceased as a boy.

A few glasses later I returned to my room. I fell asleep immediately and this time did not wake up until 9 a.m.

The Swedish girls, a Belgian couple and the rowdy Irish girls were already sitting down to breakfast. The mood in the dining room was sombre. I ordered a 'fry', ate it in silence, and an hour later checked out of the guest house. It was obviously a traumatic time for the dead man's poor family but I will never forget the endless drama.

The rest of the trip was almost an anticlimax. I explored the west coast and fell in love with it; discovered Connemara – one of the most beautiful parts of Europe; ate some delicious Atlantic seafood; and did lots of walking in glorious, lush green countryside. I also visited the Aran Islands. On one of them, Inishmore, I took a ride in a pony trap. After haggling with the driver over the price we eventually agreed that I would pay him £5 (he had originally wanted £10) but during my ride we got talking and I told him about the dead man. He was so interested in the story that at the end of the ride he invited me to the pub. He bought us both a pint, after which I offered him another. But he would have none of it and insisted on buying me two more. My drinks cost him £6 and I had only given him £5 for the ride. He introduced me to some of his friends. They had all travelled – one had worked in Boston, one in Chicago and the third had worked in New York. On this small, remote, rural Irish island we exchanged names of bars in the Bronx. I ended up having several more pints with them and at the end of our session the driver offered me a lift in his pony trap and took me back to the ferry port for free. It seemed a very relaxed approach to business and I did not see much of Inishmore.

My next visit to Ireland was a couple of years later. It was a trip for the last programme in a series so I should have expected something different. 'This weekend a famous busking festival takes place at the Irish town of Clonakilty, near Cork,' said Penny. 'And your assignment Matthew, is to take part. Come back next week and tell us how you get on.'

This one turned out to be almost as embarrassing as the nudist camp. What was I to do for an act? I couldn't sing or play an instrument. The only thing was to try a little dance.

I remembered that in the BBC North wardrobe department earlier in the summer I had seen a pith helmet. I owned a pair of DM boots and could also probably find some safari shorts and a shirt. I borrowed the helmet and went to the sound library to see if they had any Egyptian-sounding music. I decided I would try a parody of the 'Dance of the Seven Veils'.

Parody it certainly turned out to be. Being Ireland, the standard of the busking was very high. There were poets, story-tellers, Irish dancers, musicians – and me. I skipped round my tinny-sounding cassette-player which was pumping out faint Egytian music and tried to do my modest comic dance. I was heckled, whistled at and booed and when I passed round my pith helmet for contributions, two kids grabbed it and ran off. When I caught up with them they demanded a ransom for it back. I ended up in debit for my busking efforts and to make things even more embarrassing, 'The Travel Show' had sent a film crew. It turned out to be a very silly trip.

The following year I was in Ireland again – this time to do something I really fancied after reading about it in various British papers. I was sent to the south-west coastal town of Dingle to see if it was possible to swim with Fungie the dolphin.

Fungie had become an international celebrity. Spotted by local fishermen a few years before, he had returned to Dingle bay every day since. First locals and then outsiders had started to swim with him. Stories emerged of a friendship he had made with a young Irish girl to whom he even brought fish. He had become so well known that newspapers in America and even Japan had written stories about him. The result, of course, was a massive influx of tourists – something Dingle locals did not complain about.

I had read a lot of hype about the uplifting, even spiritual effect that swimming with dolphins could have on people but when I arrived in Dingle my immediate feeling was one of disappointment. All around the harbour were erstwhile fisherman offering to take tourists on dolphin trips. (Two people told me that on a good day they could make £500 – it beat going out to find a catch.) Caravans and shops sold 'I've seen Fungie' T- shirts and baseball caps, and wet suits (essential for swimming in the cold Atlantic waters) were available for hire.

I paid my £5 and went out on a boat which was laden with a group of German tourists. 'Of course, we can't guarantee you'll see the dolphin,' said the ex-fisherman cautiously after we had already been at sea for half an hour. We were about to turn back when Fungie suddenly leapt from the sea. He shot out of the water, turned a few somersaults, repeated the trick and swam off. He was visible for less than a minute but the cameras went click, the customers were satisfied and the fisherman headed back to port with a boat-load of excited, smiling passengers.

My assignment, however, was to try to swim with Fungie but the fisherman told me that this would cost at least £40, as I would have to charter a whole boat. I baulked at that and started talking to an Englishman, called Graham, who hired out wet suits from a caravan. He told me he had an inflatable raft and that he could take me for £10.

At dusk I drove to the other caravan where he lived, put on a wet suit, and along with two other young tourists set out to sea in the raft. Graham made a few circles round the bay (he said Fungie was attracted by the noise of the outboard motor) and then we jumped off the raft into the cold, dark, choppy Atlantic. We bobbed up and down in the sea waiting for something to happen. Nothing did. Then suddenly a huge fin approached. I felt very vulnerable as it started to circle us fast. 'How big is Fungie, Graham?' I asked nervously.

'About 700 lb and 12 feet long,' he said. 'He's enormous. Come on – get your face mask and snorkel on. Let's see if he wants to swim with us.' Graham and the other two swam out away from the raft and I reluctantly followed.

The girl cooed as Fungie came towards her. 'I touched him!' she gasped. 'He's beautiful.' But I was having trouble with my face mask – the glass was steamed up – and my snorkel was feeding me mouthfuls of salt water. I adjusted the straps and secured them to my face. Then I saw a giant friendly eye. It stared at me pensively then vanished as Fungie swam off. He looked like a living torpedo.

The dolphin did not reappear that night. 'He probably got bored,' said Graham.

I made two more trips with him after that. I didn't manage to swim with Fungie in the way I had imagined (like they do in Florida dolphinariums) but I did get very close to him and each time it was extremely exciting (I could see why some people advocate swimming with dolphins as a cure for depression – it's such an exhilarating experience). There was only one problem for me and that was that Fungie preferred females. If there was a girl in the sea he would always give her most of his attention. Some people I spoke to in Dingle (and there were many – locals and outsiders – who thought they were dolphin experts) suggested the reasons were sexual. Others said it was because women were smaller – apparently children receive even more attention.

My best meeting with Fungie was on my last day in Dingle. I had a flight at 10 o'clock from Shannon and Graham had suggested a dawn swim. We changed into our wet suits, set out for the bay and Fungie immediately appeared. He was in a playful mood. He swam around us in the sea, played with an inflatable ring and then a ball, and came within millimetres of us both. When he seemed to have had enough and was swimming away Graham had another idea. He had a surf-board which he attached to the raft with some string. Then he told me to lie on the board while he sailed the raft round in circles. We did it a couple of times and Fungie reappeared. He obviously loved the idea. He leapt out of the sea to say hello and then started hurtling over me. About 700 lb of speeding dolphin came within inches of my head and he did this at least a dozen times. After an hour's more playing he had finally had enough and swam off.

We rushed back to shore, I changed into my clothes and careered off in a mad rush to the airport. But it was too late. I missed my flight and had to wait four hours for the next one. The delay was worth every minute though.

I've been to Ireland many times now and it's somewhere I would recommend for a holiday. Obviously you won't find Spanish weather, but the countryside and the people always make it worth while. I did have one disappointment, however, a couple of years ago.

I was in Galway for a 'Travel Show Guide' to the west coast of Ireland. I discovered a wonderful shop, McDonagh's on Quay Street, where they sold some of the most delicious fresh fish I had ever tasted. The fish is so good because most of it arrives daily from the Atlantic. But this shop also smokes its fish beautifully. 'I use the finest oak chippings,' said the owner. 'I get 'em from the local undertaker. It's the only place I know they'll be good. I tried chipboard once but the glue changed the taste of the fish.'

After I interviewed him and took endless photos of his smokerie, the owner asked me if I would like to take back a whole salmon. Naturally I was delighted. His wife vacuum-packed it and I thanked them both and went to the airport.

After arriving in London, I was waiting for my suitcase in the baggage hall when Aer Lingus made an announcement. 'Would the passenger who left a salmon on the plane please go to the enquiry desk.' Nothing registered with me as I had all my hand luggage. Then it was repeated: 'Would the passenger who left the salmon on the aircraft please claim it from the enquiry desk.' Again nothing registered. Then the announcement was repeated again. I looked through all my bags (I was carrying my cameras, film, newspapers, chocolates and a bottle of Baileys for my mum) and to my horror could not find my salmon – it must have fallen out of one of the plastic bags. I went up to the enquiry desk to ask the man behind it for my fish. 'But it's already been claimed, sir,' he said. 'We made three announcements and then a lady said it was hers.'

'Which lady was it?' I demanded. Everyone was still waiting for their cases.

'That one over there,' he said. I glanced over to the baggage carousel to see a fifty-something, expensively dressed woman wearing furs, a feather hat and high-heeled shoes. She was carrying an elegant handbag and had my 20 lb vacuum-packed salmon sticking out, inelegantly, from under her arm. I approached her as she went to grab her case.

'Excuse me,' I said. 'I think there has been some mistake. I think that's my salmon you have.'

She paused for a moment and looked me in the eye. 'Oh is it darlin'?' she said. She spoke with a strong Kerry brogue. 'Oh yes, well maybe you're right.' And she thrust the fish at me and headed with her suitcase towards the customs hall.

CHAPTER TWENTY-SIX

Russia

Before the collapse of Communism I did not like going to Eastern
Europe. Food was usually dreadful, service was always slow and
getting anything done was always complicated.

Things are possibly still the same but I have had *some* enjoyable
trips there. A bargain holiday to Slonchav Briag in Bulgaria (known
to tourists as Sunny Beach) was fun. British tourists behaved like
James Bond as they trotted off quietly to do deals with waiters and
lifeguards and the blackmarket just added to the holiday's
excitement.

I had an interesting trip to Lake Ballaton in Hungary. I stayed on
a camp-site that was occupied half by West Germans and half by
Eastern Europeans. Many of the West Germans had fantastically
equipped camper vans (some with microwave ovens and colour
TVs) while the Eastern Europeans made do with ancient tents. The
West Germans ate out every night while the Eastern Europeans ate
out of tins that they had brought all the way from home. The West
Germans went nightclubbing while most Eastern Europeans stayed
on the camp-site playing card games.

Just before the Wall came down I made a trip to Berlin. I went
into the East on a tour bus and when we returned to the West the
baggage hold was examined by border guards with mirrors and
sniffer dogs. After the Wall came down I went to Rostock in East
Germany. The East Germans had just been given western marks for
their East German (or Ossie) marks and were buying anything they
could get their hands on. There were frenzied trading scenes on the
streets as West Germans (often ordinary individuals who'd loaded
up their cars and driven east) sold them clothes, sweets, TVs and

cars and laughed at their lack of consumer experience.

I had met a few Russians on my trips but still had not visited Russia. Then in 1991 'The Travel Show' sent me to Moscow. I went on a so-called 'Meet The Russians Tour'. This was with a company which, said the brochure, aimed to provide 'opportunities for people of Britain and the Soviet Union to get to know each other... to share thoughts, ideas and feelings with people who, until recently, were considered enemies'.

The idea sounded great. We were to stay in trade-union hotels (not the usual tourist ones reserved exclusively for foreigners) and meetings in Russian people's homes were promised.

We flew to Sheremetievo Airport where I had my first experience of some of the chaos in Moscow. Passengers off the British Airways flight from London waited half an hour before their bags finally appeared. When they did, it was not on the carousel marked 'London' but on another one marked 'Vienna'. The passengers from Vienna collected all their bags off a different carousel marked 'Stockholm' and the Swedes collected theirs off another one marked 'Baghdad'. (I did not hang around to see where the Iraqis collected theirs).

After clearing immigration and customs, and coming face to face, for the first time, with po-faced, uniformed officials previously considered our 'enemies', we made our way on to the tour bus and went to our trade-union hotel, 20 minutes outside the city centre.

A porter carried my luggage to my room and deposited it in the middle of my bed. 'Ten dollars,' he said smiling. I smiled back and gave him a dollar. He waited for more. I shook my head, smiled again, then dug into my pocket for some Quality Street chocolates. I gave him a handful – there were several green triangles – and he left with a smile on his face.

After a quick inspection of the room (it was small, the bed was hard and a few cockroaches crawled around in the bathroom) and a complicated encounter with the *dezurnaja* (the woman responsible for all the rooms on every two floors – she sits behind a desk in the corridor making sure guests do not sneak friends in or steal things from the rooms) about the possibility of having a bottle of water, I went downstairs for a pre-dinner meeting with the rest of the 'Meet The Russians' tour group.

There were about 20 people in our party. Most were over 50, some rather older. John, our tour leader, was retired from the mining industry. He spoke Russian and had been visiting Moscow for years.

'I'm afraid I've got a bit of bad news,' he said. 'The problem is, I'm having trouble getting hold of any of my Russian friends.' He mentioned a few names and said that all his contacts were either tied up or out of Moscow. The upshot, he explained, was that it didn't seem likely that we would meet any Russians there. Of course we would have contact with our guide, but as far as going into people's homes was concerned, this would not happen in Moscow.

I was extremely disappointed. Our three-night visit to Moscow was part of a longer 'Meet the Russians Tour'. The rest of the group was continuing on to Vladimir and Leningrad but I was only having one night in Vladimir before flying back to do the programme. They had plenty of further opportunities for east-west social encounters, but this meant that I probably wouldn't meet any Russians at all.

We entered the dining room where I experienced my first Russian hotel meal. 'You like caviar? You like champagne, sir?' the waiter kept asking between courses. 'I bring you caviar, best champagne.' Another waiter (who was not even serving our table) came over and offered tickets for the Bolshoi. 'I got best seats in the house.'

The food was not great – cabbage soup, pickled vegetables with ham and a scruffy lettuce leaf, meat pie and cake – but not quite as bad as I'd feared. A lady called Unity asked me what I was doing after dinner.

'I'm going to Red Square,' I told her. 'I've got to see it before I go to bed and besides, I want to try to meet some Russians.'

'How marvellous,' she said. 'What a good idea. How are you getting into the centre?'

'I'm going to take the Metro. I want to see the people and try out the public transport.'

'How brave,' said Unity. 'How will you read the maps?'

'I'll play it by ear.'

'And if you get lost?'

'I'll jump in a taxi.'

'How wonderful,' she said, and told some of her neighbours about my plan. 'Matthew's going to Red Square after dinner. He wants to see it before he goes to bed. And he's not even going there by taxi. He's going to take the Metro. He wants to try to meet some Russians.'

'Super,' said one of the other ladies. 'What a great idea...maybe...do you think we could come too?'

'Of course you can,' I said, not fully relishing the prospect of having my movements restricted by half a dozen elderly female tourists. 'Let's meet in the lobby in 10 minutes. I'm just going up to get my camera.'

Ten minutes later I was walking through a south-western Moscow suburb heading for the Yugo Zapadnaya Metro stop, followed by a gaggle of British ladies.

After finally obtaining some change from a station kiosk (we had all changed money in the hotel but had not been given any kopeks) we each bought a ticket. 'I say – I wish the tube in London was as cheap as this,' said Unity. 'How much is five kopeks? A quarter of a penny – that's not bad at all, is it?' We took the escalator down and waited for the train to arrive.

The Metro stations in Moscow are one particular Soviet success. Stalin designed them to be 'palaces of the working classes' in the 1930s and some, like Mayakovskaya, and Smolenskaya Ploshchad, are beautiful – full of sculptures, mosaics and paintings. When I was there the trains were clean, punctual and safe (things are a bit more hectic now) but the problem for us newly arrived Brits, was how to read the Metro station names. They were all in Cyrillic and none of us knew any Russian.

After half an hour on one train, and still not sure whether we were going in the right direction, I tried out the dumb charm of an Englishman abroad on three scruffily dressed teenage girls who were seated opposite. 'Red Square?' I asked. 'This way is good? This train is right for Red Square?' They all started giggling then one replied. I felt stupid. I didn't have a clue what she was saying.

To the left of the teenagers was a blonde, very striking young woman. She was in her early twenties, and immaculately dressed all in turquoise. She had long, sharp, red finger-nails and a perfectly made-up face. Her cheekbones were high, her jaw was finely chiselled and her full lips were painted bright pink. While other passengers found us a source of amusement she remained elegantly detached. She sat bolt upright, kept her gaze fixed and never once looked in our direction. I watched her through the corner of my eye — she was beautiful — and, with her blue eyes, and cold, contained demeanour, looked like a fairy-tale Ice Queen.

None of the passengers seemed able to help us. A few gave advice but we didn't understand it. After several stations we came to another stop. The Ice Queen got up, walked past and spoke. 'Red Square is this way,' she announced. We jumped up and followed her, off the train, into the station and up on to the escalator out. She set a brisk pace and we rushed to keep up with her. The ladies kept asking her breathless questions. All of us were excited. We had been in Moscow for less than three hours and had already made contact with a Russian. 'Where did you learn your English?' asked Unity. 'It really is excellent you know.' The Ice Queen stayed cool, led us through the streets and pointed across the road to an onion-domed building — the Kremlin. 'That is Red Square,' she said. 'Goodbye.'

She turned away but I asked her to wait. I couldn't let our Russian escape. 'Stay a minute, please,' I said. 'You see, we're British and we're on a cultural trip and we were supposed to be meeting lots of Russians. Unfortunately all the people we were going to meet aren't in Moscow this weekend. You're the first Russian we've met so it would be nice if we could talk to you a while.'

'Yes,' said Unity. 'Just so we could say that we've talked to a Russian in Moscow.'

'What would you like to talk about?' asked the Ice Queen.

Unity and the other ladies then began to fire questions at her. What was her name? She said it was Khelga (that sounded suitably Nordic — her mother was from Lithuania); that she was a linguist (she spoke six languages — English, Spanish, French, some German, a bit of Lithuanian and Russian); that her father was a scientist and that she had travelled to France, Spain and Germany.

'What do you think of Gorbachev?' asked a lady.

'How did you like the West?' asked another.

'*Te gusta el España?*' I added, glad that I had finally got in a question. I was beginning to get irritated by the interest all the others showed in her. I was the one who had come out to meet Russians. It had been my idea to come into Red Square. I took the Metro, I asked the directions. She's my Russian really, I thought.

'*Tu hablas español tambien?*' asked Khelga, a smile flickering on her face.

'*Poco,*' I said. '*Me gusta el España. Donde has aprendido tu español?*'

She then gave me such a rapid answer, in perfect South American Spanish, that I had trouble following her, but I smiled back, pretending I'd understood every word. I'd sparked off an interest, established a personal link. I asked her another question in Spanish. I hoped it would show her that we had a few things in common.

Unity was then incredibly sweet – she mentioned to Khelga that I worked for a BBC television programme called 'The Travel Show' and that I was doing a special report on Russia. Khelga had not heard of 'The Travel Show' so she told her all about it before saying, 'Well maybe we should leave these two to have a little chat together. Don't worry about us dears. We'll wander round and get a taxi back. You have a good evening. We'll see you tomorrow, Matthew. And Khelga, if ever you come to London, here's my address and phone number.' Everyone then said goodbye to Khelga and I was left in Red Square with her on my own.

'So where did you learn such good Spanish?' I asked.

She started to explain, then I suggested that we went for a drink, 'In one of the foreign currency hotels – it's all right, I've got plenty of dollars.'

She took me to the Belgrade Hotel. We walked into the lobby past the doorman. She talked to me loudly in English about London, then once we were inside whispered: 'Russians are not allowed in these places you see – so I have to pretend I'm a foreigner.' We went to the small bar. She wanted a Coke. I ordered a Carlsberg.

'Five dollars please,' said the barman. I took out my wallet and opened it. I stared at it and remembered, with alarm.

'Khelga – you don't possibly... have any dollars on you do you? I'm really sorry. I can't believe it. I haven't got any with me. It's very stupid. Honestly I thought I was only coming out for an hour. I didn't realise I would be going to a bar ... I just... You see I left all my dollars in my room. I can't believe I've been so stupid.'

'So much for the affluent westerner,' I thought.

'How much do you want?' said Khelga, back into Ice Queen mode. She pulled out a roll of green notes and tossed a couple onto the bar.

'Where did you get all those from?' I asked.

'I worked for them of course. I always try to get paid in dollars.'

For a moment I feared the worse – that the explanation for Khelga's clothes and money was the obvious one. I had heard all about the girls who worked in the hotels, the ones who picked up foreigners for dollars – it was the easiest way to get them and Russians desperately needed hard currency. I had been so stupid. How could she have been anything else?

'I'm not working now because soon I am leaving for Germany' she said, 'but this summer I worked for an Argentinian company and they used to pay me in dollars. It's the best way.' She pulled out a packet of Marlboro and lit one with a small silver lighter. She pointed to the cigarettes: 'Dollars,' she said. She pointed to the Coke: 'Dollars again.' She pointed to her jacket: 'Dollars, of course. You can't buy anything good without dollars.'

Over more drinks, which Khelga, of course, paid for, I discovered that she had perfected her Spanish with a Chilean family who lived in Moscow. They were refugees from Pinochet. 'Very nice people,' she said. 'Journalists. And I have other foreign friends too – English, American, Spanish.' She mentioned the English names – Nick, Ruth and Kate. 'They spent a year studying Russian in Moscow.'

By the time we had finished our drinks it was nearly midnight. We left the bar and Khelga hailed a taxi. She lived near my hotel so we shared it. When she got out first, she said, 'So British gentleman – do you have dollars for the taxi?' She knew I didn't. So she gave me $2 and told me to ignore the driver if he asked for anything extra. 'Russian taxi drivers are very bad. Don't let him play games with you – okay? Goodbye then, young British gentleman.'

'Can I call you tomorrow?' I asked abruptly, anxious that she would disappear forever.

'What time?' she replied.

'Ten o'clock?' I said.

'Okay,' she agreed and wrote her number on some paper with an expensive-looking silver propelling pencil.

The following morning at breakfast everyone asked about Khelga. Some of the tour group seemed disappointed that they had not yet met a Russian. John told me that the group was having a tour round the Kremlin but I said I wanted to see Khelga. 'It's just such a great opportunity, you see. She speaks excellent English and I think she could make a great story.'

At 10 minutes to 10 I was ready at the phone, clasping my one-kopek coins. They had been difficult to acquire — I had had to ask six people for the change. I waited until one minute past and then slowly dialled Khelga's number.

A man answered the phone. 'Hello, could I speak to Khelga please?'

'Niet...' The phone was immediately slammed down.

I tried again. 'Hello... I'm sorry I don't speak Russian but could I speak to Khelga please?'

'Niet!' The phone was slammed down again.

I tried a third time. 'Hello...' But the phone was slammed down for a third time.

'Rude bugger,' I thought and went up to my room.

Half an hour later I tried again.

'Allo,' said a girl's voice. It was Khelga.

'Where have you been?' I asked. 'Who was that man on the phone? He didn't want to listen. He kept hanging up.'

'Oh, that was my father,' said Khelga. 'I'm very sorry. He complains about my friends always ringing.'

We arranged to meet at eleven thirty on Red Square outside Lenin's Mausoleum. I said I wanted to see his body and she laughed at such an obvious tourist interest. When we met up we joined a long queue. As well as foreigners there were plenty of Russians waiting to pay their respects. Khelga did not share their sense of reverence. 'You know some people have plans to turn this place into a disco or a nightclub,' she said.

'Sshhhhhhh...' said the guards as we entered.

'You know this isn't really Lenin. They have three different bodies which they swop all the time so they can keep the one on show nice and clean.'

'Sshhhhh...' said the guards to her again.

'Every four months they change all his clothes and give his bald head a good polish – that's why it's shiny. Look at all these people – it's ridiculous.'

'Ssshhhhhhhhh...' said the guards looking angry.

She smiled at them flirtatiously. We had less than 10 seconds to look at the body before the people behind us pushed us round. Guards gestured at me to take my hands out of my pockets, a woman was told to take her hat off. I thought Lenin looked like a waxwork but the emotion was more real for some. Two old women crossed themselves and their husbands looked visibly moved. 'So silly,' said Khelga. 'Look at them.' The guards hushed us out.

After Lenin, we walked past the Kremlin wall where all the Communist Party stars are buried (Stalin, Khrushchev, Brezhnev, Andropov, Chernenko and Yuri Gagarin) and then, after a quick tour of the Kremlin itself, decided it was time for some lunch. 'Let's go to McDonalds,' I said, showing what a sophisticated guy I was. In no other city in the world would I ever have made such a suggestion but I'd heard so much about the Moscow McDonalds – this pocket of capitalism in a communist state, which was so popular with the locals that some queued for hours to get in – that I wanted to see what it was like.

The queue for McDonald's was at least five times bigger than the queue for Lenin's Mausoleum. 'Don't worry,' said Khelga, 'We'll just have a word with this man,' and she approached the security guard standing at the door, then beckoned me over as he opened it.

'What did you do?' I asked her, when we were in.

'Just showed him a card which said I worked for ABC News.'

'And do you?' I asked.

'It's not even my business card – it belongs to a friend of mine. Now, do you have any money today?'

'Oh yes,' I said anxiously, 'Roubles and dollars.'

'Okay, well you get the food and I'll find a seat. The problem is people stay here for hours.' I could see what she meant – the place was hardly a fast-food restaurant as it was packed with Russians slowly savouring their burgers while others took pictures of the decor. 'Two Big Macs, two fries, two apple pies, a Coke and a coffee,' I said to probably the most cheerful McDonalds 'crew' member I had ever seen. He understood me, prepared my order and then even said, 'Have a nice day'.

'I don't believe it,' I said to Khelga, 'It's just like McDonalds in America. And the guy had a perfect New York accent.'

'That's because most people who work in McDonalds are educated. It is a privilege to work here. Everyone wants a job in McDonalds. They have physicists, teachers, mathematicians — all selling burgers in McDonalds. It was the first big American venture in Moscow — an American crew taught the Russian staff the system, so all those who work here feel westernised. The problem is that it's also very popular with the customers and they like the serviettes and the trays. People steal them all the time. They steal the straws too. They take everything home as souvenirs.'

Over lunch we talked about literature. 'Do you know Thomas Hardy?' Khelga asked. 'I love *Tess of the D'Urbervilles*. And Dickens — I love *David Copperfield*. But they are sad and both made me cry. What about Shakespeare? He is quite difficult but I have seen *Romeo and Juliet* in Russian.

She mentioned Graham Greene and Edna O'Brien. She seemed to have read more in English than me. 'All right then, Khelga,' I said, 'So you know a lot about literature but what do you know about British politics?'

'Well, you have a constitutional monarchy, a parliamentary democracy and a legislature made up of two different Houses. You have the Upper House — the House of Lords — and the Lower House — the House of Commons. The Speaker presides over the House of Commons and he sits on the woolsack because wool is what made England an important trading nation. You hold parliamentary elections every five years, or earlier if the prime minister decides, and the winning party...'

'Fine,' I said. 'Where did you learn all that?'

'I read many things but I also studied it at the university — we studied British history and the political system. I know a lot about your country.'

'Very impressive', I said, 'So what else do you know about Britain?'

'I know about your geography. You don't have real mountains but have many sets of hills — the Cambrians, the Cairngorms, the Pennines, the Pyrénées.

'The Pyrénées????!!!!'

184

'Oh, sorry — they are in Spain. What are the others? I seem to have forgotten.' Unfortunately I had forgotten them too. 'You have a population of 55 million, Edinburgh is the capital of Scotland, Cardiff is the capital of Wales and Belfast the capital of Northern Ireland. You have many rivers — the Severn, the Thames, the Clyde, the Tyne... you want me to continue? So what do you know about MY country then? Do you like Russian literature and music?'

'I've read *Anna Karenina*,' I said.

'You like Tolstoy?'

'Well, yes I liked that one...'

'What about *War and Peace*?'

'No I haven't managed that yet. My mother's read it though and the BBC serialised it on television. They do a lot of classical drama.

'What about Pushkin?'

'No, I don't know any Pushkin.'

'You don't know any Pushkin? How is it possible not to know Pushkin?... *Eugenio Onegin*? You don't know this poem?..' and she rattled off a few lines in Russian before translating into English... "I loved you once, And probably somewhere in my heart I still do." How can someone not know Pushkin?' I apologised with a shrug of my shoulders.

'Are you familiar with Arbat?' she then asked.

'Oh God,' I thought, 'Another obscure Russian poet.'

'No, I haven't read any Arbat either.'

'What?' she said, 'Read any Arbat?' repeating me sarcastically. 'You don't READ Arbat — it's a street, one of the most famous in Moscow. You know Montmartre in Paris? This is the Russian equivalent. It's a very nice street; no cars are allowed; it's full of painters and eccentric people; you can buy lots of things there — jewellery, military clothing, *matrioshki* (you know *matrioshki?* these are the Russian painted dolls), and — MOST IMPORTANT — Pushkin used to live there. Come on — finish your apple pie — I'll take you to Arbat Street now.'

Stopping for a minute to pose for a photo with a cardboard cut-out of Gorbachev (it cost five dollars to take the picture with my own camera) we went directly to Arbat Street. 'You like it?' she asked. 'The buildings date back to the eighteenth and nineteenth centuries.' And she showed me the house that Pushkin once lived in. 'He was here with his wife Natalia, but then she left him for a French soldier. They had a dual and Pushkin died.'

We stayed at Arbat Street until some drunken Russian sailors arrived. They started arguing, then fighting so we got into a taxi and went to the Intourist Hotel where the bar was full of American and Korean businessmen. They were almost outnumbered by prostitutes. The young, pretty girls wearing skin-tight clothes sauntered around smiling in front of them until every now and then one of the men would catch their eyes and a girl would come and sit down next to him.

The next day was Saturday and in the morning Khelga took me first to Gorky Park (it was full of Russian soldiers playing on the fair-ground); back to Red Square (that was full of newly married couples eating chocolates and drinking champagne); and then up to Leninskiye Gory (Lenin Heights – where there was a great view of Moscow and even more newly wed couples consuming more champagne and chocolates). We had lunch in a small Georgian restaurant (one of the first to be privatised, it was expensive for Russians – the meal cost the equivalent of £3 and tasted rather like Turkish food) and then visited the Pushkin Museum (a sumptuous palace full of different works representing the history of world art – from Egyptian statues, sculptures by Michelangelo, to paintings by Picasso and Matisse).

The following day we went to Tzaritzino Cathedral, a gem of a church set in a park which had been hidden from the Russian people for decades, then we went to see some of Khelga's friends for lunch, and in the afternoon took a train to Peredelkino where we visited Boris Pasternak's house.

Not once did I use the Metro with Khelga. Most of the time we travelled by taxi and if none was available she just stuck her hand out and hailed a private car. She then offered the driver some hard currency, and even if where we were going was not on his way, he would invariably take us. The train back to Moscow from Peredelkino was full of Muscovites carrying bags of vegetables from the country. There were also a few drunks on board – one of whom was fighting with his wife.

We had dinner in the Intourist Hotel's Golden Hall restaurant. It paid to know the system here, as the hotel had several different bars and restaurants and some only accepted hard currency while others accepted roubles as well. The rouble restaurants were noticeably cheaper. Khelga ordered a bottle of champagne – it cost 50 roubles, less than a dollar. At the table next to ours an Italian was negotiating for some caviar.

He thought we were two British tourists. 'Crazy, crazy country,' he said.

That evening was my last in Moscow and when we finally said goodbye at two in the morning I thanked Khelga for making it one of my most exciting trips ever. We exchanged addresses and promised we would write to each other. She was leaving for Germany at the end of August (her father was of German origin and had helped her to obtain a German visa) and she said she would ring me from there.

The next morning I packed up my cases for Vladimir and met the rest of my group for breakfast in the dining room. Our coach was leaving at 10 o'clock and just before boarding I decided to give Khelga a ring. The driver started the engine but 10 minutes later I still could not find the right coins. As usual no one had any small change. Eventually a cleaner exchanged some kopeks for a couple of dollars and I raced to the phone before the coach left. 'Hi, Khelga – just to say thank you for being such a great guide to Moscow. I loved our time together and I'll try and ring you from...' But a lady from our tour group rushed in.

'Matthew – the driver's beginning to get restless and we can't wait any longer for you.'

'Okay, okay,' I said. 'Look, Khelga, I'll try to ring you from Vladimir. We're staying...'

'Matthew, please...' said the lady.

'Khelga...we're staying at the Zarya Hotel and I'll...' The phone went dead. My money had run out. I did not have time to look for more kopeks. 'Bugger, bugger, bugger,' I thought and made my way on to the coach.

It took two hours to get to Vladimir but before we checked into our hotel, our guide Valentina had decided we should first visit Suzdal, a famous ancient city, apparently full of churches. But I wasn't interested in it at all. The moment we arrived, I tried to find more kopeks and then to locate a public telephone. Unfortunately, after all this trouble, her father then answered. 'Niet!' he said and slammed it down as usual.

I made one more attempt. 'Niet!' The line went dead so I gave up and returned to the group. We were shown the churches and little country houses but I found Suzdal rather boring.

At 4 o'clock we finally checked into our Vladimir hotel. It was situated on the main road to Siberia. Apparently I had a message. 'You are Mr Collins?' asked the receptionist. 'A lady called earlier for you. Her name was Khelga. She said she would be here at four thirty.'

I returned to my room, paced round a few times, and then wandered outside the hotel. 'Boo!' said Khelga, appearing from behind a wall. 'I just caught the name of your hotel. I knew there wouldn't be many places in Vladimir so I decided to jump on the train. I took a taxi at the station and came here. The driver knew exactly where you were.'

I took her upstairs so she could wash and change and went down to tell the rest of the group that my Russian friend had unexpectedly arrived. 'She must like you then,' said one man. 'Probably just wants to marry a westerner,' suggested another more cynical chap. Unity thought it was marvellous to be seeing her again. 'How wonderful,' she said. 'Maybe she really will come to London.'

That evening there was a night of Russian singing and dancing. Khelga was made welcome by the rest of the group (who all asked her lots of different questions) and at the end of the evening I sneaked her into my room where we stayed talking until 4 a.m.

The following morning I was to be driven back to Moscow before flying back to London. A car (a Volvo belonging to Valentina's boy-friend) had been arranged to pick me up at the hotel. I was paying for it so I told Valentina that Khelga was coming too, and after a quick tour of Vladimir and goodbyes to the group, we set off.

My most vivid memories of Sheremetievo Airport that day are of having Coke and caviar sandwiches with Khelga (the restaurant had nothing else) and of an English girl and Russian boy saying a tearful farewell and promising to meet up in six months. 'How complicated,' I thought as they had a mad snog, before she finally entered the departure lounge. 'What a situation to get into.' Khelga and I enjoyed a civilised kiss goodbye, promised to write, but both of us assumed we would never see each other again.

A few days later I was on a tour of the Channel Islands for 'The Travel Show'. One night I was on Sark (one of the smallest islands) wondering what I could do to pass the time. It was 10 o'clock, I did not want to stay in my room but nor did I fancy going to a bar. The main leisure activity for most of Sark's teenagers seemed to be spending the evening in (what I remember to be) the island's only phone box. 'I know,' I thought, 'I'll see if it's free. I'll see if I can get through to Khelga.'

With a single 10p coin I got through first time. For once, her father did not answer. 'Hi, Khelga,' I shouted, 'It's...' but the money ran out and the line immediately went dead. I ran to the nearest pub, asked for as many coins as they could spare, ran back to the phone box, and armed with £15-worth of change, tried to ring Moscow again.

We chatted for over 20 minutes and a queue of local kids formed behind the box. 'Are you going to be long?' asked one, popping his head through the door.

'You'll have to wait,' I said. 'I'm on an important call to Moscow.' Khelga told me she was making final preparations for Germany (she was due to leave on 19 August and had arranged her accommodation and a job) and when I put in my final 10p coin I told her I would ring again soon. Over the following weeks I spoke to her from France, the Lake District and Walthamstow and we also exchanged several faxes (a friend let her use her company's facilities).

On the evening of 19 August I was in the bar of an Athens hotel where a television was flickering in the background. I was about to go to bed when an Italian customer changed channels. CNN news came on and to my astonishment the anchorman announced: 'Tonight the Russian people brace themselves for hard-line military dictatorship. President Mikhail Gorbachev has been overthrown in a coup in Moscow. Tanks rolled into Red Square this morning and a state of emergency has been declared.' Customers gathered around the set. I immediately thought of Khelga. I ran up to my room and tried to ring her but, unsurprisingly, could not get through. I tried ringing Germany but there was no reply from the number she had given me so I sat up until 3 a.m. watching TV and the next morning flew back to London. I took a connection up to Manchester, recorded 'The Travel Show' and was in Sardinia the next day.

'*Matteo, telefono, sempre telefono,*' said Giovanni, the taxi driver (the one who should have been a shepherd) that I was staying with. He could not understand my obsession with making calls all the time. Finally I got through to Khelga. She told me she had arrived safely but that on the day of the coup had been terrified. She had been woken up, on the day she had looked forward to for months, by tanks rolling past her apartment. 'Suddenly Moscow was full of armed soldiers,' she said. 'It was so frightening. I did not know whether I should leave. The roads were completely blocked with tanks. At the border with Poland I got out of the train to buy my last Russian newspaper but a soldier blocked my way with his gun. It's awful. My poor country. My family.'

After speaking to Khelga I phoned 'The Travel Show' producer. 'Have you booked up anything for this week yet?' I asked, 'because remember you did say you were going to let me have the weekend off? I haven't had any time at home for weeks and I really do need some rest. Please can I have a break this weekend?' He said he would consider it. 'If I don't have a rest from airports and flying I'll probably have a nervous breakdown soon. You wouldn't want that would you?' I went back to Manchester. He told me I had the weekend free and I immediately flew off to Frankfurt.

Khelga and I had the weekend together but on Monday morning I had to fly to Heathrow Airport to take a connection to Amsterdam (I was doing a cycling trip in Holland). On Sunday evening I decided that instead of going to Holland via Heathrow, I would take the train up from Frankfurt. On Monday morning I persuaded Khelga to come with me.

She had no Dutch visa and only a Soviet passport (not the easiest document in the world to travel with) but when we came to the Dutch border on the train we took out a selection of British papers and books and started talking loudly in English. The immigration men walked straight past us (and stopped a few seats further down to take off some Poles without visas) and we had two days cycling in Holland together. Khelga took my photographs and when I returned to Manchester I found, to my horror, that every one she'd taken was blurred. 'Sorry,' she said, 'I'd never used a Nikon.' We continued to write and phone and when I had finished the summer series I asked her to come and stay in London.

For Khelga to obtain a British visa I had to write a formal invitation (witnessed by a lawyer and guaranteeing her UK expenses, if necessary) which she could then show the Embassy. 'You know what you're letting yourself in for, don't you?' said the solicitor.

'Please,' I said, 'just sign the form.'

*   *   *

The climax of this story is that I've got the best possible souvenir from a trip – a family. Khelga came to see me in October 1991 and stayed and Charles Patrick Rudolph Collins (Khelga wanted his first name to be Rudolph – after her father – but I said that might cause problems for a baby born in East London just before Christmas) came into the world on 2 October 1992. Nicolai Alexander Collins arrived on 6 April 1994.